W9-CQY-648

McGinnis, Maura.
Greece : a primary
source cultural guide /
2004.
33305206699351
mi   09/01/04

GREECE

A PRIMARY SOURCE CULTURAL GUIDE

Maura McGinnis

The Rosen Publishing Group's
PowerPlus Books™

SANTA CLARA COUNTY LIBRARY

3 3305 20669 9351

For Margo, Boone, Ella, Carson, and Nora

Published in 2004 by The Rosen Publishing Group, Inc.
29 East 21st Street, New York, NY 10010

Copyright © 2004 by The Rosen Publishing Group, Inc.

First Edition

All rights reserved. No part of this book may be reproduced in any form without permission in writing from the publisher, except by a reviewer.

Library of Congress Cataloging-in-Publication Data

McGinnis, Maura.
Greece: a primary source cultural guide / by Maura McGinnis.— 1st ed.
    p. cm. — (Primary sources of world cultures)
Summary: An overview of the history and culture of Greece and its people including the geography, myths, arts, daily life, education, industry, and government, with illustrations from primary source documents.
Includes bibliographical references and index.
ISBN 0-8239-3999-5
1. Greece—Juvenile literature. [1. Greece.] I. Title. II. Series.
DF717.E447 2003
949.5—dc21

2003002243

Manufactured in the United States of America

Cover images (clockwise from left): The Temple of Apollo; a detail from the Athenian constitution written by Aristotle; and a young Greek boy in the traditional dress of the Evzone Guards.

Photo credits: cover (background), pp. 39, 58 (bottom), 80, 82 (bottom) © AKG London; cover (middle), 9 (top), 13, 25, 45, 57, 68, 70, 71 (bottom), 73, 116 (left, top right, and bottom right) © Dagli Orti/Art Archive; cover (bottom) © Stone/Getty Images; pp. 3, 116, 118 © 2002 GeoAtlas; pp. 4 (top), 9 (bottom) © Steve Vidler/SuperStock; pp. 4 (middle), 16 © Kevin Schafer/Corbis; pp. 4 (bottom), 29 © Dagli Orti/Museum der Stadt Wien/Art Archive; pp. 5 (top), 33 © Reuters NewMedia Inc./Corbis; pp. 5 (middle), 49 © Stephanie Maze/Corbis; pp. 5 (bottom), 94, 95 © Jeff Greenberg/The Image Works; p. 6 © Larry Lee Photography/Corbis; pp. 7, 48 © Scala/Art Resource; p. 8 © Yann Arthus-Bertrand/Corbis; pp. 10, 38 © James Davis/Eye Ubiquitous; p. 11 © Premium Stock/Corbis; p. 12 © M.L. Sinibaldi/Corbis; p. 14 © Photo Researchers, Inc.; p. 15 © Gail Mooney/Corbis; pp. 17, 109 © Wolfgang Kaehler/Corbis; p. 18 © Dagli Orti/Archaeological Museum Venice/Art Archive; pp. 19 (top), 36 (bottom), 79 © Dagli Orti/National Archaeological Museum Athens/Art Archive; pp. 19 (bottom), 46, 81 © Dagli Orti/Musee du Louvre Paris/Art Archive; p. 20 © Dagli Orti/Archaeological Museum Delphi/Art Archive; pp. 21, 22 © Dagli Orti/Agora Museum Athens/Art Archive; p. 23 © Dagli Orti/Archaeological Museum Syracuse/Art Archive; p. 24 © Dagli Orti/Topkapi Museum Istanbul/Art Archive; p. 26 © Dagli Orti/Mussee D'archeologie Mediterraneenne, Marseilles/Art Archive; p. 27 © Mimmo Jodice/Corbis; pp. 28, 77 © Dagli Orti/Bibliotheque des Arts Decoratifs Paris/Art Archive; pp. 30, 86 © Bettmann/Corbis; pp. 31, 34, 107 (bottom) © Margot Granitsas/The Image Works; p. 32 © Underwood & Underwood/Corbis; p. 35 © Aurora Photos; pp. 36 (top), 71 (top), 72, 74, 82 (top), 83 (bottom) © Art Archive; p. 40 © Brenda Turnnidge/Lonely Planet Images; p. 41 © Dagli Orti/Archaeological Museum Florence/Art Archive; p. 42 © Erich Lessing/Art Resource; p. 43 © Dagli Orti/Archaeological Museum Eretria/Art Archive; p. 44 © Dagli Orti/Archaelogical Museum Spina Ferrara/Art Archive; p. 47 © Dagli Orti/Biblioteca Nazionale Marciana Venice/Art Archive; p. 50 © Dimitri Messinis/AP/Wide World Photos; p. 51 © AFP; p. 52 © Adam Woolfitt/Woodfin Camp & Associates; p. 53 © Stella Hellander/Lonely Planet Images; p. 54 © Nikos Giakoumidis/AP/Wide World Photos; pp. 55, 104 © Granger Collection; p. 56 © Dagli Orti/Byzantine Museum Athens/Art Archive; pp. 58 (top), 61 © Dagli Orti/San Angelo in Formis Capua Italy/Art Archive; p. 59 © Israel Talby/Woodfin Camp & Associates; p. 60 © Paul Stepan/Photo Researchers, Inc.; p. 63 © Chris Hellier/Corbis; p. 64 © Dagli Orti/Archaeological Museum Naples/Art Archive; p. 65 © Dagli Orti/Archaeological Museum Piraeus/Art Archive; p. 66 © Dagli Orti/Bibliotheque Nationale Paris/Art Archive; p. 67 © Roger Wood/Corbis; p. 69 © Dagli Orti/ Archaeological Museum Argos/Art Archive; p. 75 © Dagli Orti/Museo de Santa Cruz/Art Archive; pp. 76, 100 © Robert Fried Photography; p. 78 © George Tsafos/Lonely Planet Images; p. 83 (top) © AKG Photo; p. 85 © Credit Visual/Matton/Corbis; p. 87 © Hulton/Archive/Getty Images; pp. 88, 97 © Lonely Planet Images; p. 89 © Jacqui Hurst/Corbis; p. 90 © Royalty-Free/Corbis; p. 91 © Ludovic Maisant/Corbis; p. 96 © David Mclain/Aurora Photos; p. 98 © Wolfgang Kunz/Bilderberg/Aurora Photos; p. 99 © Mark Honan/Lonely Planet Images; p. 101 © John G. Ross/Photo Researchers, Inc.; p. 102 © SuperStock; p. 103 © William Hubbell/Woodfin Camp & Associates; p. 106 © Suzi Moore/Woodfin Camp & Associates; p. 107 (top) © Jodi Cobb/Woodfin Camp & Associates; p. 119 © Sally A. Morgan/Ecoscene/Corbis.

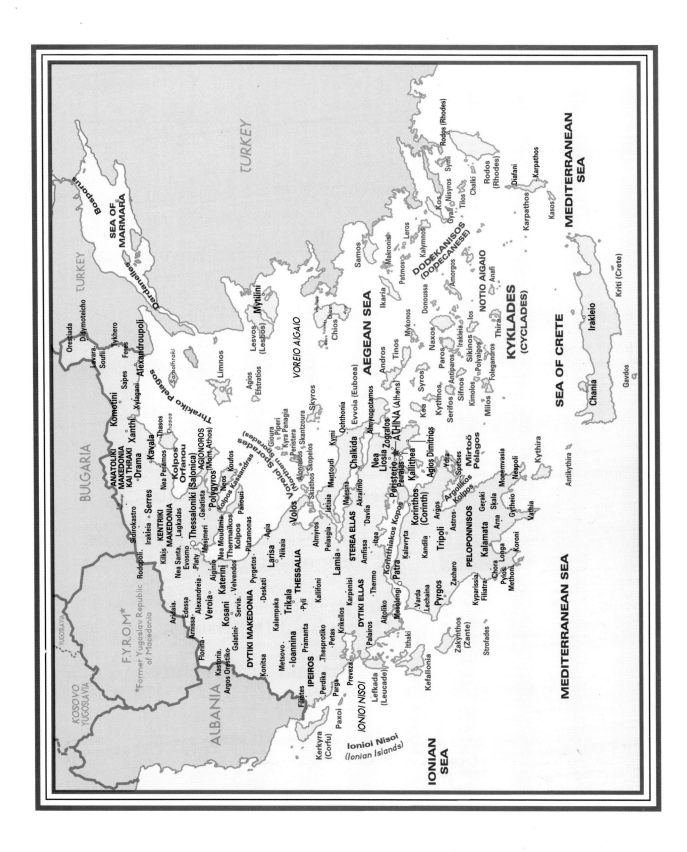

CONTENTS

INTRODUCTION

The world knows this country as Greece, which comes from the Latin word *Graecia*. Officially, it's called the Hellenic Republic and is known by its people as Helada or Hellas. This small country and its people have had a huge influence on the world. Greece is the birthplace of democracy and Western culture. In so many fields of human endeavor—government, philosophy, science, mythology, religion, and all the arts—the accomplishments and contributions of Greece have at times been equaled but have never been surpassed.

Reaching into the Mediterranean Sea on the eastern outskirts of the European continent, Greece lies at the crossroads of Europe, the Balkans, Africa, and the Middle East. The early Greeks were adventurers and traders. They took to the sea and explored the world. They imported materials, customs, ideas, and language. Always a curious and adaptable people, the Greeks absorbed new influences and transformed them into something uniquely Greek.

Being at the crossroads of so many countries also left Greece vulnerable to invasion. For centuries, barbarian tribes, Romans, Venetians, Franks, and other invaders claimed parts of Greece as their own. Its artistic and archaeological treasures were destroyed or stolen. Greek artists were forced to flee. Their exile left Greece poorer but

Athens, as seen in this aerial view *(left)*, is the capital of Greece and home to more than 4 million people. The ancient Greeks conceived of democracy 2,500 years ago in Athens, and the city served as the seat of philosophical debates about politics and art. Today, Athens is packed with busy taverns, shops, and traffic. This horse's head *(above)* from a marble sculpture of the chariot of Selene was originally located at the Parthenon in Athens. The chariot represents the moon, in Greek *selene*.

advanced and enriched the cultures of other countries. Starting in 1460, the Greek people were enslaved by the Turkish Ottoman Empire for more than 400 bitter years. Resilient and tenacious, the Greeks held on to their culture and their dream of freedom. Finally, in 1832, the Greeks reclaimed their country from the Turks and began the long, difficult road to becoming a self-governing nation.

In the modern world, Greece is a center for energy distribution. Energy-hungry nations need its oil and gas pipelines, which are located in the Balkans and Eurasia. With cultural and economic ties to the emerging nations of the region, Greece provides a diplomatic link between those nations and Western governments. And as a country governed by democratic and free market principles, it provides a stabilizing influence in this often volatile part of the world.

Travelers have always been drawn to Greece. They come for its shining past, still alive in its art and ruins. They also come to these magical islands, where the ancient sits

This village and castle are located on the island of Astypalea in the Aegean Sea. Through the ages, the island has experienced Greek, Byzantine, and Roman rule. Venice claimed it in 1207, but it then fell to the Turks in 1540. The Italians once again controlled the island from 1912 to 1945. It officially became part of Greece in 1948. Astypalea is a beautiful tourist destination with charming narrow streets and houses painted white with brightly colored doors.

The End of the Drachma

Dating back more than 2,600 years, the drachma was Europe's oldest currency. In 670 BC, soon after coinage was first developed, the drachma replaced the obol. The obol was a small iron rod. Six obols could fit into an average adult's hand. Six obols became one drachma. The world "drachma" is from the Greek *dratto*, meaning "to grasp" or "a handful." By 600 BC, the drachma was Athens's official currency. It was coined in 90 percent pure silver, weighing a little more than four grams. The first drachma was stamped with the image of an owl's head, the bird of the goddess Athena. Later, silversmiths created designs with plants, animals, gods, city views, and temples. During the years of foreign domination, the Greeks used the currency of the occupier. The drachma was reinstated in AD 1863, designed to resemble the ancient coins. The old Indian coin, the dramma, and the dirhams of North Africa and central Asia are descendants of the drachma. The adoption of the euro in 2002 was the end of the drachma.

comfortably alongside the modern, for a taste of Greek culture. Secrets of the past are everywhere, layers upon layers of civilizations waiting to be discovered. From the astounding archaeological discoveries of Heinrich Schliemann in the nineteenth century, which gave historical background to the stories and legends of poet Homer, to more recent archaeological findings, the entire world continues to learn more about the Greeks and about itself.

Greeks refer to themselves as Hellenes. They call their country Hellas and their language Hellenic. The words "Greece" and "Greek" are derived from Roman words that were used to describe the people of Hellas. Even Greeks who have settled outside their country have retained close ties with their homeland. The United States is home to approximately 2 million Greeks, the largest Greek population outside of Greece.

THE LAND

The Geography and Environment of Greece

J utting like a hand into the waters of the Mediterranean Sea, mainland Greece lies on the southern end of the Balkan Peninsula. The mainland is bordered on the west by the Ionian Sea, on the east by the Aegean Sea, and on the southeast by the Sea of Crete. There are more than 2,000 islands in these waters. Greece shares its mountainous 500-mile (805-kilometer) northern border with Albania, Macedonia (the former Yugoslav Republic of Macedonia), and Bulgaria. Turkey is its northeastern neighbor.

Greece is a small country. It has an area of 50,949 square miles (131,957 sq km), which is roughly the size of the state of Alabama. The country is divided into thirteen regions. The northern regions, including Macedonia, Thrace, and Epirus, have harsh climates with cold winters and humid summers. The regions to the south, which include Attica, Central Greece, Thessaly, the Peloponnese, and the island chains have the temperate Mediterranean climate. With hot springs, long and arid summers, and warm autumns, these regions have more than 250 days of sun. Greece has constant seismic activity. The last volcanic eruption was in 1950, but earthquakes are common and sometimes very destructive.

The Greek island of Zakynthos, seen in this aerial view *(left)*, is part of an island chain in the Ionian Sea known as Heptanesos, meaning Seven Islands. Zakynthos is the third largest island in the chain and is hailed for its beauty and artistic culture. The Tholos at Delphi *(above)* was the gateway to a sacred temple. Built in the fourth century BC, it is considered unusual because of its rounded shape.

Greece has a population of more than 10 million people. Thessaloníki and Athens are Greece's major cities. Founded in 315 BC, Thessaloníki was built on a prehistoric site dating back to 2300 BC. Now a thriving commercial and industrial port with a population of more than 1 million people, it is also a major transportation hub. Modern Athens, Greece's capital, has a population of around 3 million. The city's history dates back to settlements at least 4,000 years old. Athens is the indisputable birthplace of Western thought, culture, and democracy. Today, Athens is Greece's largest industrial center and a major tourist destination. Athens has hundreds of ancient ruins, shrines, churches, and monuments. Its many museums house ancient Greek sculptures, frescoes, and archaeological treasures.

Geographical Features

Greece has a heavily indented coastline full of coves, peninsulas, bays, and inlets. The coast is around 9,000 miles (14,484 km) long. Most of Greece's rivers and lakes are small, though several large rivers cut through the country. These rivers create fertile plains for agriculture. The Axios River is 45 miles (73 km) long. It runs down from the Balkans through Thessaloníki. Greece's longest river, Aliakmon, is 200 miles (322 km) long. It starts in the northern mountains, weaving southeast into the Thermaic Gulf. Both the Axios and Aliakmon Rivers form extensive wetlands that are home to a large variety of birds. Greece also has thousands of mineral and thermal springs. For more than 2,000 years, physicians have prescribed visits to the mineral spas for their healing benefits.

Elafonissi is a small islet on the southwest coast of Crete that is connected to Crete by a shallow reef only 3 feet (1 meter) deep. Visitors can cross the sea on foot when the water is calm. Although many tourists visit Elafonissi during the summer months, there are no permanent inhabitants.

Greece's 2,000 islands are one-fifth of the Greek landmass. Most of them are rocky specks, and less than 200 are inhabited. The Ionian Islands, the only part of Greece to escape Turkish occupation, lie to the west. In the gulf separating Attica from the Peloponnese are the tiny Saronic Islands. To the southeast lies the largest island, Crete, which was home of the ancient Minoan culture. To Crete's north lie the Cyclades, from the ancient Greek word *kyklos*, which means circle. The islands were given this name because they roughly circle the island Delos, which is the sacred birthplace and shrine of the god Apollo. The Sporades and the Dodecanese Islands lie off the coast of Turkey. Many of the inhabited islands have stupendous beaches and many archaeological and architectural treasures, including shrines, temples, Byzantine churches, Greek Orthodox monasteries, Venetian fortresses, and Turkish mosques.

Santorini, shown here, is located in the Aegean Sea and is actually a group of five islands, two of which are uninhabited. Santorini was at one time a larger, circular island, but a volcanic eruption in 1640 BC sunk its center. Still active today, the same volcano last erupted in 1950. The islands are composed of volcanic rock from eruptions over the past 2 million years. For this reason, Santorini is very dry with few springs that supply water.

Mountain ranges cover 80 percent of Greece. The largest range is the Pindus Mountains, which run like a spine down from Albania through Central Greece. The Pindus continue into the Mediterranean, where the submerged peaks form the rocky

In Greek mythology, Zeus's throne and the gods' residence were located on Mount Olympus, which was only recently associated with a specific peak. There is little information regarding the actual location of the mythological mountain; however, the tallest mountain range located on the boundary between Thessaly and Macedonia near the Aegean Sea is now known as its home.

Aegean Islands. Greece's highest peak, part of the Olympus mountains, is 9,570 feet (2,917 m) tall. Legendary home of the Greek gods, Mount Olympus is now home to an Orthodox chapel for Christian pilgrims. Rising 8,061 feet high (2,457 m) in Central Greece, Mount Parnassus shelters the ruins of the Oracle at Delphi, an ancient shrine dedicated to the god Apollo and his Oracle. The Oracle, a priestess through whom the god spoke, answered questions from pilgrims who came seeking advice. For centuries, these mountains have offered

Ecological Problems

Modern Greece is facing an ecological crisis. Rivers and lakes are polluted by industrial, agricultural, and municipal runoff. High levels of nitrates, phosphates, and pesticides contaminate the drinking water. Lakes have run dry, and rivers have shrunk from overpumping. Athenians live in a cloud of fumes from traffic and refineries. On the Acropolis, the ancient view of the sea is obscured by smog. Modern pollution has done more harm to ancient ruins than centuries of natural disasters, invasions, and looting. Rapid desertification, or the formation of deserts, is a serious threat. Much of the remaining soil is not capable of supporting plant life. With increasing forest fires, lack of drinking water, and rising temperatures, Greece is facing major ecological challenges for the future.

Greece is home to a variety of mountain goats. They live in the rugged and often sparsely vegetated higher elevations and eat plants and bushes that dot the hills. Since goats are used for the production of milk and cheese, a major industry in Greece, the government provides subsidies to people who cultivate bushes or raise goats.

refuge for humans and animals. Shrines, ruins, and monasteries cling to the rugged cliffs gazing over spectacular gorges and canyons. In the forests of the northern mountains, bears, lynxes, wolves, boars, and other wild animals have escaped extinction. Remnants of ancient European forests, with a greater diversity of trees than anywhere else in Europe, still survive in these mountains.

Animals, Plants, and Natural Resources

Greece has deer, mountain goats, jackals, foxes, and wildcats. More than 400 species of birds, including raptors, nightingales, and many game birds, make their home in Greece. The wetlands provide sanctuary for birds of the north and south, such as ibex, pygmy cormorants, shrikes, pelicans, and flamingos. Greece also offers one of the last havens for the endangered monk seal. The surrounding waters are home to octopuses, dolphins, cockles, red mullet, and nearly 300 species of marine life.

Greece is rich in native plants. More than 6,000 species have been recorded so far. The country has thousands of flowers, such as roses, anemones, orchids, rhododendrons, and violets. Edible greens and herbs, including thyme, oregano, rosemary, lavender, and dozens more, also grow wild throughout Greece. Herbs are still used medicinally by people who live in the countryside.

Greece has always had little resources, with barely enough for itself let alone for export. However, its mountains offer bauxite, lignite, lead, iron, and magnesite, and its earth is rich in limestone, clay, and marble. The marble is so fine-grained that tiny details can be etched on the surface. It has always been a coveted export. Greece is also exploring the possibility of oil in the Aegean Sea.

THE PEOPLE

The Ancient Greeks and the Modern Greeks

Greece is a country with a rich past. Evidence of its long history may be seen in its archaeology, architecture, and the many stories recounted in its literature. The world's oldest human skeleton was found in Greece, on the Halkidiki peninsula southeast of the city of Thessaloníki, in a cave named Petralona. Scientists have traced the skull back 700,000 years, the earliest Stone Age period on the European continent.

Early People

The first great civilizations in Greece were the Cycladic, Minoan, and Mycenaean people, who lived during the Bronze Age (c. 3500–1200 BC). Settling on the Cycladic Islands, the Cycladics were farmers and sailors. The sailors traded metals, gems, and crafts throughout the Mediterranean. With poor soil and limited resources, the islands could not support more growth or people. By 2200 BC,

The Acropolis *(left)*, which means "high city," is located on a steep-sided rock outcropping that overlooks Athens. The Acropolis was built in the fifth century BC, and its design was considered distasteful in its day. The Parthenon, which means "virgin's dwelling," is the city's focal point and honors Athena, the city's patron goddess. This detail of the Dolphin Fresco *(above)* is located at the Palace of Knossos in Crete. The palace, created by Minoans, is 3,500 years old and is an airy space with skylights throughout. Artfully decorated, it was not only a residential palace but also an administrative center.

The Treaty of Alliance among the cultures of Crete, Lycos, and Rhodes dates from the second century BC. After the extinction of the Minoan civilization, its history became legends in Greek tradition and mythology. Ancient Greek authors tell of King Minos, for whom the culture is named, who was a wise lawmaker, judge, and dominator of the sea.

the Cycladic culture was peacefully absorbed by its southern neighbors, the Minoans.

The Minoans, a dark Mediterranean people, had settled on Crete. They had a great navy and traded throughout the Mediterranean. On Crete, there were no fortifications and few weapons. The Minoans built complex, sophisticated palaces with indoor plumbing, an innovation that would not be seen elsewhere for centuries. Ruins of their art, buildings, and inventions tell of a peaceful, creative people who loved beauty, nature, sport, and celebration.

After 2100 BC, a northern Indo-European people invaded the mainland. A warrior culture, they had chariots, long swords, and different gods than the people they conquered. These people, later known as the Mycenaeans, easily overwhelmed the existing farming settlements. They built grim citadels throughout Central Greece and the Peloponnese. The Mycenaeans also furthered their culture by trading with and colonizing other regions surrounding the Aegean Sea.

This gold death mask of Agamemnon dates from between 1580 and 1500 BC and was excavated in 1876 by archaeologist Heinrich Schliemann. He believed the gold mask to be that of Agamemnon, legendary king of Mycenae, although the mask dates from 300 years before the Trojan War supposedly took place. Schliemann was looking for the grave of Agamemnon, who led the forces against Troy to win back Helen for King Menelaus.

By 1600 BC, the Mycenaeans had come in contact with the Minoans and adopted aspects of their culture. Later, the Mycenaeans sacked Minoan cities. The Minoans rebuilt, but within fifty years, their civilization was mysteriously and completely destroyed. Around this time, a volcanic eruption blew the island of Santorini to pieces. Scientists think the eruption, followed by earthquakes and tidal waves, had a worldwide effect. It is possible this eruption wiped out the Minoan civilization. Minoan excavations show signs of fire and flood but no signs of fighting or invasion.

Around 1200 BC, the fair and blue-eyed Dorian tribe invaded Greece from the north. With superior iron weapons, they overpowered the Mycenaeans. The Dorians settled in the Peloponnese islands and Crete. They also sailed to Asia Minor (Turkey) and its offshore islands. Another tribe, the Ionians, settled in Central Greece and the Aegean Islands. It appears that there was a low population between 1050 and 900 BC, which means that many Greeks probably moved away to avoid invaders or lack of water and food. Unfortunately for historians, writing and the arts ceased during this period. Because so little is known about it, this time in Greece is called the Dark Ages.

Historians have pieced together much of what we know about the early Greek people, before the Dark Ages,

This fifth-century BC vase depicts Odysseus using a stake to put out the eye of Cyclops. Odysseus was a great fighter in the Trojan War. After the war, Athena, goddess of war, created obstacles for Odysseus to make it difficult for him to return home. Odysseus stopped at Sicily, the island of Cyclops, and became trapped in Cyclops's cave. Odysseus and his men escaped by stabbing Cyclops in the eye and hiding among sheep that were let out to pasture in the morning.

The Charioteer of Delphi was discovered in the Temple of Apollo at Delphi and dates from 474 BC. The charioteer is part of a larger sculpture that was erected to commemorate the victory of a chariot race. The statue does not celebrate the charioteer but rather the owner of the chariot and the team of four horses.

based partly on poems by a Greek man named Homer. Homer, who probably lived around the ninth century, told of these early people in his epic poems, *The Iliad* and *The Odyssey*. For centuries, most readers considered his stories complete fantasy. For a few, though, Homer's stories were a map to a lost world. Beginning in the nineteenth century, using Homer as his guide, Heinrich Schliemann, a German financier, began the search for these early people. At sites in Asia Minor, Attica, and Crete, Schliemann and others unearthed the hidden ruins of the early civilizations. Digging continues, there and elsewhere, and discoveries are made all the time.

The Rise of the Polis, the City-State

In the seventh century BC, Greece began to emerge from the Dark Ages. There was renewed trading and colonization. This was the beginning of the Archaic Period (650–480 BC). Oligarchies, or rule

by a small group of aristocrats, replaced monarchies. The scattered people gathered into self-contained communities that were partially defined by natural boundaries of mountains and water. Each polis, or city-state, consisted of an urban center and the surrounding territory. Each had its own character, government, laws, army, and constitution. The city-states worshiped the same gods, but they did so in their own way.

The most powerful city-states were Sparta and Athens. Settled by the Dorians, Sparta was a severe, militaristic oligarchy with a powerful army. It was a closed society, where only those of Dorian blood could be citizens. Athens, on the other hand, welcomed new people, ideas, and influences. By 730 BC, the city was the cultural center of Greece.

Inscribed potsherds, called *ostraka*, were used as ballots in the process known as ostracism. When there was a fear of tyranny, Athenians voted to exile politicians who were considered dangerous to democracy. If more than 6,000 votes were cast, the man whose name appeared in the majority was sentenced to a ten-year exile. These tablets date from the fifth century BC and are inscribed with names of prominent Athenian politicians such as Themistocles and Aristides.

Athens was also the first society in history to establish a democracy. Democracy, from the Greek *demokratia*, means "rule by the people." In the sixth century BC, two Athenian aristocrats, Solon, and later, Cleisthenes, introduced radical political reforms. They peacefully broke the stranglehold of the landed classes. These two shrewd, visionary leaders created a government where all free men were citizens. All citizens were equal before the law, with equal rights and protections.

This marble fragment of the bottom of a *kleroterion* dates from the third century BC. The kleroterion was a lottery machine used to select jurors. On the court date, a large group of jurors arrived, each carrying a bronze ticket with his name, his father's name, and his tribe's name inscribed on it. Each potential juror's ticket was placed in a slot in the kleroterion. The magistrate who presided over the procedure then dropped black and white marbles into a funnel that ran down the length of the machine. If a marble came up white, all jurors in the corresponding row were selected for service. If it was black, that row of jurors was dismissed. This process continued until the required number of jurors—about 200 per case— were selected.

In ancient Athens, only free adult men could be citizens. Slaves and women were excluded. Educated slaves served as tutors or scribes, while the most unfortunate labored in the Athenian silver mines. Some slaves received wages and eventually bought their freedom and became citizens. Though Greek culture depended on slave labor, the practice was regarded with mixed feelings. The Spartans had a huge population of slaves, whom they treated harshly. Many Athenians were uncomfortable with slavery but found reasons to justify it. Others were vehemently opposed to it, denouncing slavery as evil. To be a woman in ancient Greece was not much better than being a slave, and in one way it was worse. A woman could never, under any circumstances, become a citizen. Young girls were married as teens to men who were often twice their age. They were expected to stay at home, quietly serve their husbands, rear their children, and excel at the domestic arts. Very few women escaped this

This statue, possibly of Demeter, goddess of grain, dates from between the sixth and fifth centuries BC. Greek myth associates the cult of Demeter with the city of Enna, high in the mountains of central Sicily. During the sixth and fifth centuries BC, Sicily and the lower peninsula of Italy were completely colonized by the Greeks. This region was known as Magna Graecia, or Great Greece to the Romans.

confined role. Orphans, priestesses, and prostitutes were the exception. Very rarely, a woman might receive a good education and become a teacher.

Classical Greece

After surviving two invasions by the Persians, Athens experienced a golden age that spanned fifty years. This was the beginning of the classical period, which lasted from 480 to 323 BC. There was an explosion of creativity at the highest level in all the arts. During this time, a leading general, Pericles, also initiated further democratic reforms. The Athenians believed that democracy depended on each man's contribution to the community and each man's ability to govern himself. A democracy was not possible unless the citizens took

وقال يعمل صورة سولوز على الصفه المذكوره ويأمله

This Turkish manuscript illustration depicts Athenian statesman, lawyer, and poet Solon in discussion with students of political science. Solon was elected as a chief archon, or officer of the state, and instituted many political, economical, and social reforms. At the time he took office in 594 BC, the nobles held most of the land and political power, and peasants were losing their land and freedoms. Solon annulled all mortgages and debts and limited the amount of land any one person could own. He also outlawed all loans that would force a person to pledge his liberty as collateral, ending serfdom. Solon established a humane law code, which replaced a harsher code that sought the death penalty for even minor offenses.

great personal responsibility. A person of character was a person of *sophrosune*. This is a complex word that means respecting inner laws of balance, harmony, and proportion. The Athenians believed a truly free man was a self-governed man.

Despite Pericles' great efforts, the balance of power and influence shifted toward the wealthy. Athens became increasingly imperialistic, which led to the Peloponnesian War. In his great book, *The Peloponnesian War*, the Greek historian Thucydides sadly recorded the breakdown of values in Greek culture. Moderation was now despised as weakness, and recklessness and scheming were admired. Political ties were more important than family ties. Involving almost all of Greece for twenty-seven years, the war left the entire country weak and depleted.

The Battles of Marathon and Salamis

In 490 BC, 10,000 Athenian citizen-soldiers and 1,000 allies stood near the beach of Marathon to face more than 100,000 Persians. The Athenians were armed with spears and had no cavalry. The Persians had cavalry, wicker shields, spears, archers, battle-axes, iron-studded clubs, and bullwhips strong enough to break a man's neck. The Athenians swiftly charged, their spears crashing into the wicker shields. They bent the Persian forces into a V, pressing them into each other. The trapped Persian army was shoved into the sea. Most of them escaped, but 6,000 Persians died. The Athenian army lost 192 men. A runner brought the news of victory to Athens. Today, the origin of the word "marathon," meaning a long-distance race, can be traced back to the Greeks.

The Tumulus of Marathon, in Attica, Greece, was erected in 490 BC to mark the ancient battlegrounds.

In 480 BC, Persian forces invaded Athens and sacked the Acropolis. They massacred or took as slaves all those who hadn't fled. Confident in victory, the huge Persian navy was moored in the narrow Straits of Salamis. The tiny, agile Athenian navy bushwhacked the Persian ships, turning their superior size and numbers against them in the narrow straits. The Persian navy was decimated.

Empires

In 338 BC, Philip of Macedonia conquered Greece. After he was assassinated, his son, Alexander the Great, took over the throne. Alexander was one of the greatest generals in history. Alexander loved Greek culture and envisioned a Hellenized world. During the

The style of a particular piece of pottery often denotes the region from which it originated. The oil flask in this photograph dates from between 475 and 420 BC and depicts a seated woman plaiting a wreath.

first part of the Hellenic period, from 330 to 300 BC, he spread Greek culture throughout his enormous empire. He created Greek-speaking cities throughout Europe, the north coast of Africa, Persia, and into Asia. After Alexander's death in 323 BC, his generals divided his empire. Poor and shrunken, Greece was no longer a political power. By 146 BC, it was a province of the Roman Empire. For the next twenty centuries, Greece would be invaded or ruled by other powers.

However, its cultural influence continued. The Romans devoured Greek culture. The Byzantine Empire, which was the eastern part of the Roman Empire, spoke Greek and considered itself Greek. Arab and Irish scribes translated Greek poetry, philosophy, and scientific writings. They carried their translations throughout Europe and the Mediterranean. Fleeing invaders, Greek philosophers, writers, and artists immigrated to Europe and influenced the Renaissance. Venice had a special quarter, or section of the city, for Greek immigrants and sponsored Greek studies at the university.

Even though some Greek exiles found a new home and respect, they had lost their country. *Xentia* is a Greek word that means both "love" and "loss of native land." For a Greek, exile was the most painful loss imaginable.

In 1460, the Turkish Ottoman Empire conquered Greece. The Turks called the Greeks *rajah,* meaning "cattle." They were forced to work the estates of the Turkish

military leaders. They had to pay a head tax or their heads would be removed. Each family had to give up a son for the Turkish army, and beautiful daughters were taken for Turkish harems. When the Ottoman Empire was facing revolt elsewhere, they considered exterminating the Greeks.

Independence

On March 25, 1821, the War of Independence began. In 1832, the Greeks reclaimed their devastated and impoverished country. For the next hundred years, Greece was a pawn in the schemes of European powers. A succession of foreign nobles were crowned or elected. The Cretan statesman Eleuthérios Venizélos was the father of modern Greece. He became the prime minister of the country in 1910. Devoted to the idea of a free and whole Greece, he almost bloodlessly reconstructed the nation. In World War II, which was fought between 1939 and 1945, the Greeks fought heroically on

This detail of the ancient Roman mosaic *Battle of Issus* shows Alexander the Great on his horse, Bucephalus, rushing forward to attack the Persian King Darius III, marking a turning point in their conflict. The king was easily spotted as he drove a gold chariot onto the battlefield, and Alexander charged straight for him. King Darius III panicked at the sight and fled. When the Persian troops saw their king fleeing, they immediately collapsed and were sent into disarray. Alexander won the battle and expanded his empire.

the Allied side with the United States and the United Kingdom. Occupied by Italians, Germans, and Bulgarians, Greece during the war was a place of incredible hardship. In Athens alone, more than 40,000 people starved.

The horrors of World War II were almost eclipsed by the years of civil war in Greece, which began in 1944 and continued until 1949. During two Communist rebellions, neighbor turned against neighbor, brother against brother. Both sides of the conflict were guilty of unspeakable horrors. After surviving centuries of foreign domination, tightly knit communities unraveled.

After 1949, Greece was relatively stable. In the 1960s, political unrest returned. A junta, which means "rule by the military," took over the government. This was a harsh, repressive regime. In 1974, the junta was removed. A new constitution was written, and

This engraving *(left)* shows a Greek revolutionary raising the flag of rebellion. On March 25, 1821, Bishop Germanos of Patras hoisted the Greek flag at the monastery of Agia in Peloponnese in an act that marked the beginning of the Greek War of Independence. Fighting began in Peloponnese and quickly spread to the mainland and surrounding islands. Although the Greeks were severely outnumbered by the Turkish forces, their battle cry became "Liberty or Death." The war ended in 1829 because of diplomatic and military intervention by other Europeans. This is a painting of the Battle of Navarino *(above)*, which took place on October 20, 1827. On this day, the European fleet of France, England, and Russia sailed into Navarino Bay to confront the Turkish-Egyptian fleet. An Egyptian vessel fired on an English ship, and cannon fire immediately began. In the end, many of the Muslim ships were destroyed and thousands died. The European powers suffered few casualties or damage.

These Gypsies socialize at a market in Athens. Greece is home to nearly 300,000 Gypsies, who are an underprivileged minority in the country. The Gypsies' attempts to settle down are thwarted by prejudices, increasing land prices, and illegal eviction. Recently, the government implemented programs to provide them with adequate housing, jobs, literacy programs, and other social services.

Greece was declared a parliamentary republic. Finally, after more than 2,000 years, true democracy returned to Greece.

The Greeks have always been passionate, quick to anger, and incredibly individualistic. Yet, except for the periods of civil war, when the country was threatened, they could unite for a common cause and accomplish the impossible. Bishops, priests, poets, and farmers took on the roles of politicians, diplomats, soldiers, and freedom fighters. During the years of oppression under the Turks, the World War II occupiers, and the junta, the Greeks had to exploit all aspects of their character to stay alive as a people and as a culture. They needed slyness, deviousness, and above all, humor. Wit and humor were a form of passive resistance. And throughout their history, the Greeks have displayed astounding courage, ingenuity, and resilience.

Over the centuries, many of the invaders were gradually absorbed into Greek culture and society. There is a small community of Romas, or Gypsies, and some

This photograph *(left)* shows Turkish paratroopers invading the Greek island of Cyprus on July 20, 1974. Turkey tried to justify the invasion of 40,000 Turkish troops as a peace mission to establish order after a Greek military coup took place. However, after their mission was accomplished, the Turks remained. Their goal was to colonize Cyprus as the first measure in annexing the island. They seized the north of the island and forced 200,000 Greek Cypriots to leave their homes. Since 1974, 65,000 mainland Turks have been relocated to Cyprus to change its population ratio. On November 18, 1983, the north of Cyprus was declared the Turkish Republic of North Cyprus, a state no other country but Turkey recognizes. Today, a border established by the Turkish government in 1974, the so-called Green Line, divides the island in two zones.

Eleuthérios Venizélos

The great patriot Eleuthérios Venizélos (1864–1936) almost single-handedly reconstructed Greece as a country. A brillian negotiator and strategist, he served on and off as Greece's prime minister between 1910 and 1933. Through artful alliances and treaties, Venizélos reclaimed Crete, Thrace, much of Epirus, Macedonia, and most of the Aegean Islands from the Ottoman Empire. He nearly doubled Greece's territory

and population. Venizélos devoted his life to what he called "the Great Idea," or the political union of all Greeks in the Mediterranean region. He successfully negoti-ated with the Turks for the return of almost 2 million Greeks living in Turkey in exchange for 400,000 Turks living in Greece. Venizélos initi-ated reforms in educa-tion, agriculture, and the court system. He tried to build a demo-

Eleuthérios Venizélos *(center)* signs a treaty of peace with Italy as Benito Mussolini *(right)* looks over his shoulder. This undated photograph was taken in Rome, Italy.

cratic government but was thwarted by the impatience of his own sup-porters and the opposition of reactionary forces. In and out of political favor, Venizélos always returned when his country called upon him. His long life ended in exile in Paris, where he still wrote letters urging oppo-nents to cooperate with each other. Even in death his enemies feared him. The dictator Metaxas forbade Venizélos's body to lie in state in Athens. He was afraid there would be a riot.

Turkish people as well. There are some Albanians, Armenians, and other Balkan people. There is also a sizable undocumented immigrant population from the Balkans. According to the government, Greece is 98 percent Greek, almost everyone speaks Greek, and 98 percent of the population practices the Greek Orthodox religion. Greece is the most ethnically homogeneous country in Europe.

This married Greek couple sit waiting outside of a polling place in Athens. In the past, men and women had different roles in the family. Women primarily focused on taking care of the family and home while men provided food and shelter. However, as more women enter the workforce, these roles are changing. The one aspect of Greek family structure that remains the same is the father's position as the head of the household.

1

ΝΙΚΟΣ ΚΑΣΕΡΗΣ
NIKOS KASSERIS

ΦΩΤΟΓΡΑΦΟΣ   1ος Οροφος
PHOTOGRAPHER   ☎ 31857
   2543

RHODES IMAGE
INSTANT
ΔΙΑΦΗΜΙΣΤΙΚΗ ΦΩΤΟΓΡΑΦΙΑ
ADVERTISING PHOTOGRAPHY
ΕΚΔΟΣΕΙΣ - ΕΝΤΥΠΑ - SLIDES - ΔΙΑΦΑΝΕΙΕΣ
ΑΝΤΙΓΡΑΦΕΣ - ΠΛΑΣΤΙΚΟΠΟΙΗΣΕΙΣ - ΒΙΒΛΙΟΔΕΣΙΕΣ

ΜΙΚΡΟΒΙΟΛΟΓΙΚΟ - ΒΙΟΧΗΜΙΚΟ
& ΑΙΜΑΤΟΛΟΓΙΚΟ ΕΡΓΑΣΤΗΡΙΟ
ΙΩΑΝΝΗ ΑΝ. ΜΗΝΕΤΤΟΥ
ΙΑΤΡΟΥ ΜΙΚΡΟΒΙΟΛΟΓΟΥ
ΑΙΜΟΛΗΨΙΑ   ΑΠΑΝΤΗΣΕΙΣ
07:30 - 13:30   17:30 - 20:30

ΚΑΡΑΧΑΛΙΟΣ ΣΩΤΗΡΙΟΣ
ΧΕΙΡΟΥΡΓΟΣ - ΟΦΘΑΛΜΙΑΤΡΟΣ
ΔΕΧΕΤΑΙ ΚΑΘΗΜ. 9-1 & 5-8
ΤΕΤΑΡΤΗ   9-1
ΕΚΤΟΣ ΣΑΒΒΑΤΟΥ   ☎ 28 953 & 23244

2

ΚΩΤΗΣ ΑΛΕΞΑΝΔΡΟΣ
ΙΑΤΡΟΣ ΕΣΥ
ΑΠΕΙΚΟΝΙΣΤΗΣ - ΑΚΤΙΝΟΔΙΑΓΝΩΣΤΗΣ
ΓΕΝ. ΝΟΜΑΡΧΙΑΚΟΥ ΝΟΣΟΚΟΜΕΙΟΥ
ΡΟΔΟΥ   ΤΗΛ. 67600

"ΕΘΝΙΚΗ„
ΑΣΦΑΛΙΣΤΙΚΗ
Ασφαλειες Ζωης
ΤΗΛ. 34586   2ος ΟΡΟΦΟΣ

3

ΓΙΩΡΓΟΣ Κ. ΤΣΑΡΟΥΧΑΣ
ΟΙΚΟΝΟΜΟΛΟΓΟΣ

ΣΤΕΡΓΟΣ Θ. ΑΛΑΒΑΝΟΣ
ΔΙΚΗΓΟΡΟΣ
3ος ΟΡΟΦΟΣ   ΤΗΛ. 28521
STERGOS T. ALAVANOS
ATTORNEY AT LAW
3rd Floor   TEL. 28521

ΤΕΧΝΙΚΟ ΓΡΑΦΕΙΟ
ΚΑΡΑΒΕΛΑΤΖΗΣ Γ.
ΠΟΛΙΤΙΚΟΣ ΜΗΧΑΝΙΚΟΣ
ΤΗΛ. 37836   3ας ΟΡΟΦΟΣ

ΑΘΑΝΑΣΙΑ ΖΗΣΙΜΟΥ - ΚΑΛΑΕΝΤΖΗ
ΔΙΚΑΣΤΙΚΗ ΕΠΙΜΕΛΗΤΡΙΑ
ΠΡΩΤΟΔΙΚΕΙΟΥ ΡΟΔΟΥ

THE LANGUAGES OF GREECE

3

From Ancient Greek to Modern Greek

Greek is the oldest European language. Descended from the Indo-European branch of languages, spoken Greek is almost four thousand years old. Rich, supple, and resilient, the Greek language is the forerunner of all Western languages. One-sixth of the words in the English language have Greek origins. It is the language of philosophy, education, the sciences, the arts, and technology.

In excavations of Minoan and Mycenaean ruins, archaeologists discovered stone tablets inscribed with script. The Minoan tablets were inscribed with a script called Linear A, and the Mycenaean tablets were inscribed with a script called Linear B. For years, the scripts were indecipherable. In 1952, military code-breaking techniques were used to decipher the Linear B script. It was a very early form of Greek. Even though experts think Linear A is also a form of early Greek, this has yet to be proved.

Writing, Dialects, and Koine

During the Greek Dark Ages, the skill of writing was lost. Traveling bards, or poets, preserved history, myths, and legends orally. In the ninth century BC, near the end of the Dark Ages, writing was rediscovered. The Greeks adopted the alphabet of the Phoenicians, a seafaring people from the

Signs at the entrance to an office building on the island of Rhodes *(left)* are written in both Greek and English. Although Greek is the official language of the country, many people speak Italian, English, German, or French. A man *(above)* reads a Greek newspaper. The Greek alphabet differs from the Roman alphabet in that there are twenty-four letters. Many of the Greek characters such as pi and sigma are used as math symbols throughout the world.

The Phaistos Disc is a circular clay tablet found at the ruins of the Minoan Palace of Phaistos. The tablet is inscribed with 242 signs used only by the Minoan people and written in Linear A, a script that has yet to be deciphered. In Linear A script, although the writing developed from hieroglyphic pictures, the pictograms actually represent syllables.

eastern Mediterranean. They took the sixteen symbols for the Phoenicians' consonants. They changed them only slightly, such as *alpha* for the Phoenician *alep*, and *beta* for the Phoenician *beth*. The Phoenician alphabet did not have vowels. The Greeks added vowel sounds; *a*, *e*, short and long *i*, *o*, and *u*.

In the Archaic Period, there were four major Greek dialects. These were Arcado-Cyprian, Dorian, Aeolian, and Ionian. The dialects were only slightly different, and people could easily understand each other. The mainland dialects merged into the Attic of the Athenians and the Dorian of the Spartans. Since Athens was the cultural and political center of Greece, the Attic dialect, also known as classical Greek, became the dominant dialect. By 403 BC, the Greeks had adopted the Ionic script, which was read from left to right and top to bottom, as is English.

Alexander the Great carried the use of Attic Greek throughout his huge empire. In Europe, northern Africa, the Middle East, and Asia, to speak Greek was to be a civilized person of education.

This stone tablet featuring Linear B script was found at the Mycenaean Pylos Palace of King Nestor. Linear B has eighty-nine phonetic characters. Many Linear B tablets found at Pylos warn of an attack from the sea.

The new Greek-speaking people influenced the language and a new dialect, called Koine, evolved. Koine, meaning "common" or "shared," was a simpler, suppler form of Attic Greek. Koine thrived from 300 BC to AD 300. Much of the Bible's New Testament and other Christian texts were written in Koine. It replaced Latin as the language of the Byzantine Empire. However, the Byzantine elite and scholars thought Koine too lowly for their use. They continued to use Attic Greek, which they considered pure and correct.

During Turkish domination, almost all of Greek culture and language completely froze. Ruled by the Venetians, Crete was the only part of Greece to experience the Renaissance. Cretan arts and language were strong, vital, and open to new influences. The beginnings of the modern Greek language began in seventeenth-century Crete. In 1669, the Turks invaded Crete, and its writers fled to the Ionian Islands. There, the Cretan writers were exposed to new forms of writing and speaking. Remote mountain regions also eluded the Turks, so their language and folk cultures continued to develop.

Demotic

After independence, Greece reached into the past to recapture its old greatness. In 1834, Katharevousa, a purified form of Attic Greek, was declared the official language. Most writers rejected Katharevousa as stiff, artificial, and dead. They promoted the demotic, meaning the "language of the people." This was the dialect born in seventeenth-century Crete and nourished on the Ionian Islands. Descended from Koine, demotic had absorbed influences from

English Words from Greek

democracy	*demokratia, demos* meaning "people," *kratien*, meaning "to rule"
history	*historia*, meaning "learning by inquiry" or "narrative"
icon	*ikon*, meaning "image," "figure," or "likeness"
iconoclasm	*ikon* meaning "image," *klasma* meaning "broken," together meaning "image-smashing"
metropolis	mother city, *meter* means "mother," *polis* means "city"
micro-	*mikros*, meaning "small"
mega-	*megas*, meaning "big"
monks	*monos*, meaning "alone"
museum	from Mouseion, "House of the Muses"
poet	*poietes*, meaning "one who makes"
telephone	*tele* means "far off," *phone* means "sound"

Greek Words and English Pronunciations

Good morning/Good day	Kalimera	(kah-lee-MEH-ra)
Good evening	Kalispera	(kah-lee-SPEH-ra)
Please	Parakalo	(pah-rah-kah-LO)
Yes	Ne	(NEH)
No	Ohi	(O-hee)
Thank you	Efharisto	(ef-hah-ree-STOH)
Good health!	Stin ygia sas!	(STEEN ee-YAH SASS!)
I'm sorry	Lipame	(lee-PAH-mee)
Excuse me	Signomi	(sig-NO-mee)
Good	Kalo	(kah-LOH)
What time is it?	Ti ora ine?	(TEE O-rah EE-neh?)
I don't understand	Den katalaveno	(THEN kah-tah-lah-VEH-no)

folk songs, European languages, and Albanian and Slavic immigrants. For the next 142 years, Greeks argued, debated, and fought, sometimes even violently, about language.

Katharevousa remained the official language. The Orthodox Church used Koine, as it still does today. In the most remote

This statue of Dionysios Solomós stands outside a museum on the Ionian island of Zakynthos. Solomós (1798–1857) is Greece's national poet, and his poem "Hymn to Liberty" became the Greek national anthem, "Hymn to Freedom." He led the nineteenth-century artistic movement that chose demotic as the preferred language and refused to use classical Greek. Demotic became the official language in 1976.

Giorgos Seferis (1900–1971) excelled in literature and politics. During World War II, he accompanied the free Greek government in exile to Crete, Egypt, and Italy. He returned to Greece in 1944 and became an ambassador to Turkey, England, Lebanon, Syria, and Iraq. Seferis's travels are the setting for his writings, which deal with alienation, wandering, and death.

regions, old dialects were spoken and can still be heard. The fierce Mani, direct descendants of the Spartans, still speak a dialect from the ancient Dorian. But the poets, writers, and common people wrote and spoke in demotic. In 1976, demotic became the official language of Greece.

From the Ionian island of Zante, the writer Dionysios Solomós was influenced by European culture, the exiled Cretan poets, and folk songs. He had early success writing poetry in Italian, but he gave up Italian to forge the new Greek language. In his *Dialogue Between the Poet and the Pedant Scholar*, Solomós wrote, "Is there anything in my mind but liberty and language?" He challenged writers to "submit to the language of the people, and if you are strong enough, conquer it."

In 1963, poet Giorgos Seferis became the first Greek poet to win the Nobel Prize in literature. In his Nobel lecture, Seferis praised Solomós as "a fervent partisan of popular language . . . He loved the living language and worked all his life to raise it to the level of poetry of which he dreamt."

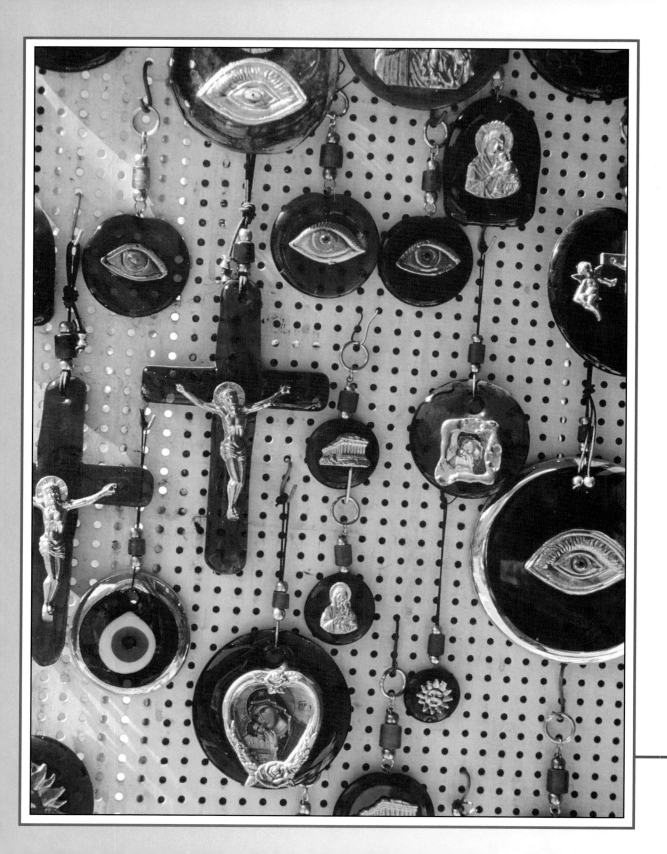

GREEK MYTHS AND LEGENDS

4

Myths and legends are traditional stories of gods, heroes, strange creatures, and monsters. Sometimes the stories are believed to be factual, but often there is little or no evidence to prove this is so. However, myths always have some truth, because they reveal something about the people who created them.

Through myths, man explained how his world was created. Myths might explain the weather, volcanoes, or earthquakes. Early man's discoveries, inventions, and crafts could be explained by myths, or myths might represent feelings or energies. Myths also explained certain events in life, such as birth, death, marriage, and war.

The ancient Greeks believed that gods and mythical creatures were everywhere. The gods of the underworld lived in caves and subterranean passages. The jagged peaks of Mount Olympus were home to the great Olympic gods. Hades, the god of the dead, lived in the Underworld. There were thousands of lesser gods. The satyr Pan, half man, half goat, lurked with other satyrs in caves and grottoes. Nymphs and Nereids, some of the female divinities, inhabited every tree, spring, river, valley, and mountain.

These religious icons, crosses, and *matia (left)* are for sale in Athens. A *mati* is a blue charm in the form of an eye that is believed to ward off the "evil eye," or bad luck. It is used as a protective talisman. Every person has his or her own mati and it cannot be borrowed or lent. This bronze statue is of the wounded Chimera *(above)*, a character from Greek mythology. The Chimera was an animal that had a lion's body, a serpent's tail, and a goat's head emerging from its back. This statue depicts the dying Chimera after it was slain by the Greek hero Bellerophon.

This bas-relief from the east frieze of the Parthenon depicts the Greek gods Apollo and Poseidon. Poseidon was the god of the sea, known to create islands and calm seas, as well as cause shipwrecks, earthquakes, and drownings. Apollo was worshiped as the god of the sun. Temples at Delphi and on the island of Delos were dedicated to him.

The Gods

The earliest Greek myths told of the birth of the universe. First, there was only Chaos, a dark vast space. Chaos created Night and Erebus, a dark place under the earth. Night and Erebus combined and created Day and Ether, the substance that fills space. Gaea was Earth. Lonely, she created Uranus, the sky, and together they created the mountains and the seas. Gaea and Uranus had many children including the twelve Titans and many misshapen, monstrous creatures. Uranus imprisoned the ugly children in caves and mountains. Gaea grieved for them and tried to turn her other children against Uranus. She persuaded her son Cronus to kill his father. Cronus married his sister Rhea, and their children became the Olympic gods, who formed the basis of Greek mythology.

The Olympic gods were the gods of the Myceneans. The gods were anthropomorphic, meaning they had the shapes and characteristics of humans. They were huge, brawling, lusty individualists, a glorified image of the Greek people. Almost always astoundingly beautiful, the gods had extraordinary powers and lived forever.

These gods were also patriarchal, meaning male deities were more powerful and influential than female deities. The early farming communities and the Minoan and Cycladic civilizations had fertility goddesses. The Olympic gods overshadowed and absorbed the fertility goddesses of the older cultures. Most of the Olympic goddesses have roots as fertility goddesses, but they lost some of their power and influence.

The Olympic gods and goddesses lived on Mount Olympus. Other than demanding worship, most of the gods were not that interested in mankind. Only one human failing was certain to get their attention and that was hubris, or arrogant and excessive pride.

This terra-cotta centaur was found broken in two parts, each placed in a different grave. Centaurs have the body of a horse and the torso, head, and arms of a man. Gods and mortals ostracized them because of their lustfulness and drunkenness, but centaurs are credited with teaching Greek heroes how to ride horses and use the bow and arrow.

Only the gods were allowed to be proud. Hubris was punished by Nemesis, the goddess of vengeful destruction.

Zeus and his brothers and sisters were the first generation of Olympians. Zeus was father of the gods and mortals. God of thunder and ruler of the sky, he was also the god of justice and weather. Zeus had hundreds of children, some divine, some mortal. Hera was his wife and his sister. She was the goddess of marriage and the protector of women. Zeus gave the seas and shores to his brother Poseidon and the Underworld to his brother Hades. Demeter, with roots as an ancient fertility goddess, was the goddess of fruits, grains, and the harvest. The keeper of hearth and home, Hestia, was an aunt to Zeus. The quietest and oldest deity on Mount Olympus, she was not the most powerful, but she was the most venerated by the Greeks.

Zeus's children were the second generation of Olympians. Son of Zeus and Hera, Hephaestus was the divine blacksmith. He was the god of fire and metalworking, and patron of arts and crafts. His forge, which was in a volcano, threw fire and smoke into the air, even causing eruptions. He was the only Olympic god who was ugly and lame. The gods and Greeks regarded ugliness as a personal fault. Although his lack of physical beauty caused the other gods to treat him poorly, he married Aphrodite, goddess of

The Greek god Dionysius, the god of wine, is depicted on this vase. During the Dark Ages of Greece, the cult of Dionysius spread quickly, especially among women. The followers were known as maenads (mad women), and while they experienced their religious frenzy, they sometimes tore apart people and animals, believing that they were devouring the god. The maenads tended to be lawless and noisy and worshiped Dionysius by dancing wildly.

love and desire. An ancient fertility goddess, some sources make her a daughter of Zeus. Homer said she arose from the white foam of the ocean, blown by Zephyrus, the west wind. Not only was Aphrodite beautiful, but she had the seductive power to make everyone feel beautiful.

Zeus's other Olympic sons were Ares, Hermes, and Dionysus. The god of war, rage, and brutal courage, Ares fought only for the thrill of slaughter and destruction. Though careful not to ignore Ares, the Athenians viewed him with some distaste. He was most honored in warlike Thrace and Sparta. Hermes, the messenger of the gods, had many functions. The god of travelers, commerce, and shepherds, he was also associated with wisdom, medicine, magic, and prophecy. The god of wine and nature, Dionysus, represented liberation from control. His followers were wild raving women called the maenads. They worshiped him with shrieking and wild dancing.

Apollo

Apollo's temples at Delphi (shown below) and on the island of Delos were two of the most sacred shrines in the Greek world. As the god of healing, music, and the arts, Apollo brought many gifts to the Greeks. His semidivine son, Asclepius, was a physician-priest and teacher to Hippocrates, the first mortal physician. The ancient Hippocratic oath, still sworn by modern doctors, says: "I swear by Apollo Physician and Asclepius and Hygeia and Panaceia and all the gods and goddesses . . . " As the god of music and the arts, Apollo was attended by the nine Muses. The Muses were nymphs, and each one represented an artistic discipline such as epic poetry, dance, or music.

Intellectual, spiritual, and rational, Apollo represented moderation, order, harmony, and formal perfection. "Know thyself" was inscribed on his temple at Delphi. Apollo is also said to be the origi-nator of other Greek axioms: "Moderation in all things" and "Nothing in excess." Apollo represented the classical ideal of balance and proportion.

The twins, Apollo and Artemis, were the children of Zeus and the nymph Leto. Apollo was the god of light, healing, music, and prophecy. His twin, Artemis, was the virgin goddess of the moon and the hunt. She was also the protector of wild and newborn creatures. As a goddess of the forests, she preferred to live in the woods and rarely visited Mount Olympus. Artemis also had roots as a fertility goddess.

Zeus's last daughter, Athena, was the warrior goddess of wisdom, peace, learning, and crafts. Athena and Poseidon competed to be the patron of Athens. Each was to give a gift to the city, and the gods would judge the best gift. Striking his trident spear against the Acropolis, Poseidon created a saltwater spring. Athena's gift was the olive tree, which provided shade, food, oil, and fuel. The gods judged Athena's gift best. A mortal,

This Greek cup from the sixth century BC portrays Amphytrite, Athena, and Theseus. Amphytrite, the wife of Poseidon and the sea goddess, was confined to the sea and was rarely associated with her husband. Athena, goddess of war and wisdom, is usually depicted in full armor and a helmet. Theseus was a king and hero of Athens, best known for killing the Minotaur, a creature that required the sacrifice of seven boys and seven girls every nine years.

Ariachne, boasted that she was a greater weaver than Athena. The goddess challenged Ariachne to a contest of weaving and won. Athena punished Ariachne for her hubris in thinking she could weave as well as a goddess. As punishment, Athena turned Ariachne into a spider.

The gods' ruined temples and shrines still stand throughout Greece. On the island of Delos, stone lions guard the remains of the temple to Apollo, and some of the ancient theaters, which were temples to Dionysus, are still in use. On the island of Corfu, there are remains of ancient temples to Artemis, Aphrodite, and Hermes. In Argos stands the original foundation of a shrine to the Great Goddess, an old fertility goddess. In the mountains, some say strange Pan-like creatures still threaten the flocks of shepherds.

Other Creatures

Along with the gods and goddesses, the Greeks also believed in many mythical creatures. The ancient monster Chimera was a fire-breathing she-goat with a lion's head.

The sixteenth-century illustration was taken from a Greek manuscript that depicts the Basilisk, a mythological snake-like creature said to be the king of serpents. The Basilisk had the ability to burn everything it approached and kill with a mere glance. It had natural enemies such as the weasel, which was immune to its glance, and the cock, which killed with the sound of its crow. Even seeing only a reflection of the Basilisk could literally frighten an animal to death. Although a mythological creature, it is believed to be factually based on either the horned adder snake or the hooded cobra of India.

ὄφις κδ̄ ᾱ

† περὶ ὄφεως κδ̄ ᾱ

Δηός ἐῖς ἱππόκραγες ἀκριβῶς ὄφις .
ἐπικεφαλῇ γαυριῶν κ̣ρασοφόρῳ .
τὸν ἄνδρα δάκων, τῆς πνοῆς ὑπεξάγη .
εἴ γαν ἐπ' ἀυτῷ δὶς φοροῦ τι περακλέ
τ̣ καὶ δαφνοὶ . τῶς γὰρ ἄγεωνον πάδο
ὁ κὰ ἄπαξ ἔρρευσεν ἐς τῆ κ̣ρδίαν .
ἢ τῷ ἰαδῶν ἐκπεφαύλισαι κρίσις ;
δρ ἢ νόσος παρῆλθε ἐ τοῖς σοῖς ὅροις ;
τῶ ἀφορισμῷ ἐς κ̣ωὸν πεφευσομ̣ων
ἐἰοῖς . κ̣αφ̣ᾶς σ πρί ἐσοι δ̄μ̣ων ː

Pictured is a statue of Zeus, the divine king of Greek mythology. The worshiping of Zeus originated with the Minoan people who referred to him as the Earthshaker. Zeus came to embody Greek religious ideals, especially in literature. He was known as a protector of the king, brought peace in times of violence, maintained laws, and gave prophecies.

Twin sea monsters, Scylla and Charybdis, were a deadly team. A treacherous whirlpool, Charybdis capsized ships. Scylla, meaning "she who rends," had six dog heads and devoured the drowning sailors. Centaurs were ancient creatures believed to be half horse and half human. The centaur Chiron was educated by Apollo and Artemis. Schooled in music, medicine, and prophecy, he was a wise teacher to many Greek heroes and demigods. After his death, Chiron became a constellation in the sky.

The Fates were three sisters. Protectors of women and marriage, they also determined a person's destiny. In ancient times, even Zeus had to honor their decisions. In remote villages, young women about to be married still leave offerings for the Fates. They hope the Fates will bring them children. When a child is born, some families still put out a plate of milk and honey to appease the Fates.

Superstitions

The Greeks are a deeply superstitious people. When speaking of children, Greeks conclude with a solemn wish for their welfare. Children are considered especially vulnerable to the workings of the "evil eye." The evil eye is a vague negative force connected to envy. There are blue glass charms, carried or worn as jewelry, to repel the evil eye. Even in modern times, some Greeks carry or wear garlic to protect themselves against the evil eye. Hung in some homes and businesses, garlic is a protection

This vendor holds a garlic braid. Greeks use garlic to ward off evil and bad luck, believing that demons and evil spirits fear it. In ancient Greece, garlic was left at crossroads to prevent the ill will of Hecate, goddess of witchcraft. Today garlic is worn on clothes and hung in the home.

against bad luck. Some Greeks believe that when one's right hand is itchy, money will be lost. If the left hand is itchy, money will be gained. If both hands are itchy, money will be gained and lost. When Greeks see a priest, they often kiss his hands or clothing. However, if they see the priest in the street, it is considered bad luck. They spit three times into their shirt or a handkerchief. The handkerchief is kept knotted until the end of the day to keep the bad luck from escaping. Greeks will never begin anything new on Tuesday. Ever since 1453, when Byzantium fell to the Turks on a Tuesday, the day has been considered bad luck.

Greeks also believe that the twelve days between Christmas and Epiphany are the most active time for supernatural beings. Some of these beings are considered to be the descendants of the satyrs and centaurs. There are the harmless pygmy Kallikantzaroi who play pranks. The giant Kallikantzaroi, though, are more dangerous, according to Greek superstition. Large, black, hairy creatures with red faces and tongues, they have monkey arms and goat legs. At night, they come down chimneys. They defile cooking pots and jump on sleeping people, scaring them witless. During the day, these creatures return to the earth. To protect the home, the hearth fire must always burn, and pots must be cleaned by hot coals.

GREEK FESTIVALS AND CEREMONIES OF ANTIQUITY AND TODAY

5

The Greeks have always loved rituals, ceremonies, festivals, and cultural events. Festivals celebrate their common history and identity as citizens and Christians. Modern Greeks have a festival for every day of the year and more pagan festivals than do any other Christian people.

Modern Christian festivals resemble ancient celebrations. There are often long ritual processions accompanied by pipes, horns, drums, and in modern times, the pealing of church bells. An icon, an image representing the religious figure being honored, is carried through the streets to the church or shrine.

Epiphany

Beginning at Christmas, Epiphany is a twelve-day holiday of parties and gift giving. On Christmas Eve, children go from house to house singing carols. Neighbors give them dried fruit, nuts, sweets, and gifts. Christmas is a quiet family occasion. Saint Basil's Day is the New Year's celebration. Saint Basil is celebrated for his love of children and generosity to the poor. Gifts are exchanged and a special cake, *vassilopita*, is served at midnight. A gold coin is baked inside the cake, and whoever is served the piece with the coin will have good luck for the new year. The last day, the Feast of Epiphany,

Fireworks *(left)* shoot from behind the Parthenon as Greece celebrates New Year. Many Greek families play cards and other games of luck until after midnight when people often wish one another "Many happy returns!" A man holds up a crucifix *(above)* after catching it during the traditional ceremony of blessing the water on Epiphany Day, January 6. Many swimmers join in the festivities on this day by jumping into the cold water and competing for the cross, which is believed to bring health and happiness to the person who first catches it.

is the blessing of the waters. All seas, lakes, rivers, and springs are blessed. To symbolize Christ's baptism, boaters, sailors, and their vessels are doused with water.

Carnival, Lent, and Easter

Easter, a celebration of joy, hope, love, and eternity, is the most holy Greek Orthodox holiday. It is preceded by almost nine weeks of other celebrations and religious days. In March, heralds proclaim the start of Carnival. Celebrated for three weeks, Carnival is a raucous music-filled time of parades, spontaneous street processions, masquerade parties, and cultural events. On the island of Skyros, Carnival resembles an ancient Dionysian festival. Young men wear goat masks, hairy jackets, and copper goat bells. Clanging their bells, they strut through town trailing a man dressed as a goat bride. The last day of Carnival, called Clean Monday or Shrove Monday, is for picnics. Greeks eat a lot of garlic and onions, an ancient practice thought to protect against the devil. Clean

Monday is followed by Lent, a forty-day period representing Christ's time in the wilderness. This is a time of fasting and subdued spirits. Most Greeks fast only the first and last weeks, while devout Greeks fast the entire Lenten period. (They abstain from eating any animal products.) Easter preparations begin the last week of Lent. Eggs are boiled and dyed red to symbolize the blood of Christ. On Holy Friday, a representation of Christ's body covered with flowers is carried in a street procession. A sweet braided Easter bread is baked with red eggs woven into the braids. The following night, on Holy Saturday, everyone attends church for a midnight Easter service, where

Greek Orthodox services mark every Easter Sunday with an afternoon mass called the Great Vespers of Agape. During this service, the gospel is read in various languages. Afterwards, Greeks celebrate the holiday with large feasts that include a roasted lamb, which symbolizes Jesus' sacrifice for his people.

each member of the congregation holds an unlit candle. Just before midnight, the church is plunged into darkness, except for the light of the everlasting flame. As the clock strikes twelve, the priest lights his candle and calls for the faithful to do the same from his flame. Upon returning home, Greeks break their fast with a midnight meal.

Other Festivals

On March 25, Greeks observe two holidays. The Day of the Annunciation celebrates the archangel Gabriel's appearance to the Virgin Mary. On this day, he announced the coming of a special child. Greeks also celebrate Independence Day on this date. Celebrated with military parades, Independence Day marks the beginning of the Greek revolt against the Turks. In 1821, an Orthodox bishop raised the Greek flag at his monastery in Peloponnese. He called for the Greeks of the Peloponnese to rise against the Turks. March 25 was chosen for this act of rebellion. The Day of Annunciation and

Greek soldiers carry a portrait of the Virgin Mary through the streets of the island of Lipsi in the procession to honor Panagia Harou, the Virgin of Death. The icon depicts Mary cradling the inanimate body of the crucified Jesus. It is for this reason that the icon became known as the Virgin of Death.

A firewalker strides across smoldering coals during the three-day celebration of Saints Catherine and Helen. Firewalkers prepare for the moment by dancing to hypnotic rhythmic music in order to achieve a trance-like state. Practitioners run back and forth on the coals while holding religious icons, which they believe will protect them from getting burned.

Independence Day both celebrate the birth of a new spirit.

In Greece, every day of the year celebrates a male and female saint. Most Greeks are named for a saint, and they celebrate the day of the year dedicated to the saint from whom they took their name. This is called a name day. Almost every town, village, city, and island has a patron saint, and the inhabitants celebrate their saint's day. On the Ionian island of Zante, Saint Dionysios is the island's patron saint. He is celebrated on August 24 and December 17. The saint's remains, some bones, and clothing are paraded through the streets. Believers who are hoping to be healed lay in the street so the saint's remains will be carried over them.

In northern Greece, Saint Catherine and Saint Helen are honored in late May with the Anastenaria Firewalking Festival. This festival also celebrates a miraculous rescue. In 1250, villagers rushed into their burning church to rescue icons, and no one was harmed by the flames. The festival begins with the sacrifice of a sheep. To the music of a lyre and a bass drum, the villagers, carrying icons, dance in procession. To the pounding of the drum, the villagers walk on hot coals to symbolize what happened in the church. Afterward, the villagers feast until dawn.

The Olympic Games

The ancient Olympics were a religious festival to honor Zeus at his shrine in Olympia. Open to all Greeks, it was a spiritual and cultural celebration. The Olympics featured competitions in sports, music, and poetry. Every four years, wars and hostilities were suspended to allow spectators, athletes, and other participants to travel to Olympia.

In the spirit of the ancient festival, the Greek government is now trying to establish a new Olympic tradition. Since the 2000 Sydney Olympics, Greece has been hosting an international cultural festival celebrating body, mind, and spirit. The Greek government hopes future host countries will continue to sponsor a Cultural Olympiad in the years between the Olympic games.

This vase from the sixth century BC depicts an Olympic victor being crowned. Winners of the ancient Olympics games received crowns made from olive branches and were entitled to have statues of themselves erected at Olympia. Victors brought their city fame and often obtained benefits such as meals paid at the public's expense and front-row seats at the theater.

THE RELIGIONS OF GREECE THROUGHOUT ITS HISTORY

6

There are thousands of Greek Orthodox churches throughout Greece. It is the official religion of Greece. According to the government, it is practiced by 98 percent of the Greek people. Under the Greek constitution there is religious freedom, but Greek Orthodox is the only religion protected and financially supported by the government. It has enormous economic and political power.

Every village is centered around its silver-domed Greek Orthodox church, which has deep ties to the community. The Greek Orthodox Church has a long history of social philanthropy. It runs hospitals, homes for the elderly, orphanages, hospices, and schools. Church leaders have been active in the pursuit of social reform. Throughout Greece's troubled history, bishops, monks, and priests have risked and lost their lives in the fight for freedom. It was the Church that sustained the Greek people through the centuries of Turkish domination. Believing it is a Christian responsibility to care for the earth, church leaders today are active in the search for answers to Greece's ecological problems. Nuns are trained in new agricultural techniques and teach local farmers to better use and conserve their land. The Church has founded the World Fellowship of

Virgin and Child (left), a painting by Greek artist Emmanuel Zane, dates from the seventeenth century. Greek Orthodox is the prevailing religion in Greece and is the only religion in the country protected by the government. The Church maintains a strong presence in the community and influences the daily lives of Greeks. However, people retain their non-Christian superstitions such as not leaving scissors open so people will not talk behind their backs. *Panagia Gorgoepikoos (above)* is a twelfth-century church in Athens that was built on the ruins of an ancient temple dedicated to the goddess Eileithyia.

This fresco depicts Christ Pantocrator and four Evangelists and archangels. "Pantocrator" means "Ruler of All," and it is this imposing image of a stern Christ that is painted on the interior central dome of most Orthodox churches. Christ is always shown at the highest point in the church so that there is a sense of him overseeing his believers.

Orthodox Youth, which sponsors spiritual and ecological work camps. The groups learn practical conservation techniques. They also restore and maintain traditional footpaths and shrines.

Beliefs

The faithful believe the Orthodox Church is the pure original Christian Church. They believe in the Holy Scripture, or the Bible, as the source of revelation and religious understanding, and they practice the seven Sacraments given by Jesus Christ. They believe in the Holy Tradition, which is the Holy Scripture and the writings and teachings of apostles, saints, martyrs, and fathers of the Church. The Holy Tradition also includes the oral tradition of the early Church and all collective wisdom and experience from Church history. Followers believe in one god, the Holy Spirit, and God's son, Jesus Christ, who was born of the Holy Spirit and the Virgin Mary. Orthodox prayer vows the people's belief in the Crucifixion, the Resurrection, and Christ's ascension into Heaven.

This illustration from the Psalm of David is dated 1066. The Book of Psalms is divided into 150 chapters, two-thirds of which are attributed to David. The chapters are numbered differently in Hebrew and Greek manuscripts. Protestants use the Hebrew version, while Catholic and Orthodox translations are based on the Greek manuscript.

Baptism is the most important day in the life of an Orthodox Christian. The priest dips the baby three times in the baptismal water, symbolizing Christ's three days in the tomb. He then cuts three locks of hair from the child. After the ceremony, relatives wish the parents "Na sas zisi," meaning, "Life to the baby."

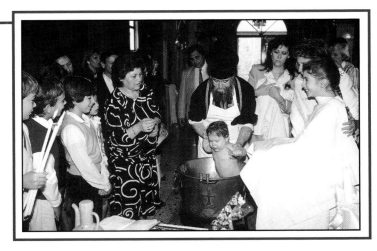

The Greek Orthodox Church and the Roman Catholic Church share the same seven Sacraments. These are baptism, confirmation, the Eucharist, confession, the Holy Orders, marriage, and Holy Unction. In baptism, a person is immersed in water to cleanse away sin. Confirmation is when a believer takes on full membership in the Church. The Eucharist is Holy Communion, or taking wine and bread that symbolize Christ's blood and body. In confession, the faithful confess their sins and repent, or ask forgiveness. The Holy Orders refer to clergymen. Marriage is a sacrament where two people become one in spirit. Holy Unction is the forgiveness of sins and the healing of the body. During this sacrament, the sick and dying are anointed with holy oil, representing the healing grace of God.

Holy Orders

The archbishop is the leader of the Greek Orthodox Church of Athens. He has authority over central and southern Greece. The patriarch of the Constantinople Church presides over northern Greece. There are bishops, monks, nuns, and priests. The bishops cannot marry so that they can devote themselves completely to the Church. They offer practical and spiritual advice. Their districts are small so they can have personal contact with the parishioners. Monks and nuns, who also cannot marry, live in the community, in monasteries, or as hermits. Priests, who can marry, are elected by the parishioners and live in the community.

Split of the Early Christian Church

The Orthodox Church was once the eastern part of the early Christian Church. As head of the Western Christian Church in the eleventh century, the pope of Rome

Greek Orthodox priests are bearded and wear long black robes and cylindrical hats. They are allowed to marry and raise children as long as the marriage occurred before they make their vows to the church. Priests, or *papás*, are highly respected in the Greek culture.

declared himself the absolute authority in all matters concerning the Church. The head of the Eastern Church, the patriarch, refused to accept his authority. The pope excommunicated him, which means he was excluded from all rights, sacraments, and privileges of the Church. In 1054, the Christian religion split into two different churches, the Holy Roman Church led by the pope, and the Orthodox Church headed by the patriarch. For centuries, the Roman Church would not recognize the Orthodox Church. It was not until 1967, almost 1,000 years later, that the pope met with the patriarch. In recent years, the two leaders have been on friendly terms but continue to differ on various religious issues.

The Orthodox Church does not believe in the infallibility of the pope or the patriarch. Neither Christ nor the early Christian leaders gave this power to any church leader. The patriarch is considered the first among equals, but no greater than any of his bishops or followers. As Christ's apostles were equal, so are all laymen, priests, and bishops. Unlike in the Roman Church, Orthodox priests can marry, and the Eastern Church uses leavened bread for Communion. The branches of the Orthodox Church, such as Greek Orthodox or Russian Orthodox, are self-governing units. The Orthodox Church celebrates God's love and man's nobility. The Roman Church focuses on God's justice and man's original sin.

History

Jesus was Jewish and followed Jewish tradition. This included the belief in monotheism, the Old Testament, and righteousness. However, Jesus also preached of new

This fresco dating from 1072 *(right)* depicts the miracle of Jesus curing a blind man. Statues are banned in the Greek Orthodox Church as the Greek clergy decreed that only God is worthy of being worshiped. Instead, Greeks pay their respect and honor to God through icons. Icon paintings depict the lives of Jesus and the saints and are often covered with gold and silver that reveal only the painted face and hands of Jesus or the saint. Icons emphasize Christ as a human, and many are displayed in Greek homes, offices, shops, cars, and buses as reminders of the values and virtues Greeks must pursue.

ideas concerning love, forgiveness, and salvation. As he became more influential, many people began to see Jesus as the long-awaited Jewish Messiah, the Anointed One. The Romans and some Jews feared him as radical threat. Arrested on a false charge, Jesus was condemned to die by crucifixion.

As Christian tradition has it, Jesus, now dead, was taken down from the cross and given to his followers. He was put in a cave and then his body disappeared. His followers searched vainly for his body. Christians believe that Jesus rose from the dead, proving his divinity and his eternal message.

Jesus' apostles and followers fanned out through the Mediterranean to preach the gospel, meaning the "Good News." In the first century AD, Saint Paul, an apostle of Jesus and a Greek-speaking Jew, came to Athens. He stood on the Acropolis and preached about God's love and forgiveness. In Asia Minor, when Saint Paul tried to speak, he was mobbed and imprisoned. The Athenians, ever curious, welcomed him and listened. They were very receptive to the new teachings. Saint Paul set up Christian communities throughout Greece until he was beheaded by the Romans.

Many of the early Christians were Greeks or people who had become Hellenized. In the fourth century, Alexander the Great had Hellenized the Mediterranean area. To be Hellenized was to adopt or be influenced by the Greek language, customs, and culture. Most of the New Testament of the Christian Bible was first written in Greek. For the first eight centuries of its existence, Christian doctrine was defined by Greek or Hellenized writers and philosophers.

The Christian gospel was similar in spirit to the teachings of these philosophers and writers. The gospel did not define goodness, truth, or even God. It was for every man to search for himself. Phrases from the gospel, such as "Seek and ye shall find" and "The truth shall set you free" were mirrored in the teachings of the great Greek philosophers.

Philosophy

For the ancient Greeks, philosophy was a form of contemplation or prayer. In Greek, *philos* means "loving" and *sophia* means "wisdom," so philosophy means "love of wisdom." Philosophers reflected on the meaning of life, goodness, truth, and the eternal. They discussed ethical questions of right and wrong, duty, and destiny. Plato, Aristotle, and many other Greek philosophers wrote extensively and some had schools, in which students learned to reason, think critically, and discuss ideas. In 387 BC, Plato founded a school, the Academy, that lasted for 1,000 years. The Academy was not intended to

Meteora

The Holy Trinity Monastery in Meteora, Greece.

The Meteora, Greek for "hanging between Heaven and Earth," are twisting rock pinnacles rising out of the northwest plains of Thessaly. These sandstone formations, 2,000 feet (610 meters) high, are the home of Orthodox nuns and monks. During times of persecution, monks found refuge on the Meteora. They built the Hanging Monasteries, which are medieval monastic communities that cling to the cliffs. Legend has it that in 1340, the first monk reached the Great Meteora on the back of an eagle. By 1500, there were twenty-four monasteries, accessible only by ropes, pulleys, and drawbridges. Today there are five, including two nunneries. Now there are rough roads and steep steps cut into the rock. The monasteries house many priceless ancient manuscripts, icons, Byzantine frescoes, and religious artifacts. The monks and nuns tend the gardens and sound the bells. Spending their time in contemplation, their lives have hardly changed in centuries. With the exception of tourists, the modern world barely intrudes.

enshrine a set of truths or beliefs. Like true democracy, all ideas were open for discussion and debate. It served as a model for schools throughout the Hellenic world. During the Renaissance, a new Academy, based on Plato's school, was founded in Florence. The work of the Greek philosophers is the foundation of Western thought.

Plato started out as the student of another great philosopher, the Athenian Socrates. If Socrates wrote down his thoughts, nothing he wrote has survived.

Socrates (470–399 BC) is portrayed in a bust of marble. Socrates was an ancient Greek philosopher known for his strong moral beliefs. Mistrusted by many Athenians, Socrates had distinct religious views and often encouraged youths to question ancient traditions and authority. At the age of seventy, he was convicted of atheism (belief that there is no god), treason, and corruption of youth.

Nonetheless, many people recorded his influential teachings, particularly his student Plato.

Socrates believed wisdom, goodness, and truth were real and attainable, but only through a personal search. Even though he was realistic about his faults and the faults of others, Socrates had an optimistic belief in man's essential goodness. He believed evil came from ignorance and anyone who knew what was good would do it. His method of teaching was to constantly question. By questioning his students, he hoped to awaken a longing in them to search for truth and goodness.

Monotheism and Polytheism

In Greece, it was Socrates who led the transition to monotheism. The worship of the Olympian gods was a form of anthropomorphic polytheism. Polytheism, which means the worship of many gods, was adaptable and tolerant of new gods, rites, and ideas. Monotheism, which demanded the worship of only one god, was the only threat. Instead of the humanlike Olympian gods, Socrates conceived that there existed a single god as pure spirit, in and above nature. Despite his impeccable reputation, Socrates was tried for impiety and corruption of the young. He could either deny his thoughts or be executed. He chose death.

By the fifth century BC, Zeus had become the divine authority. The other gods were still honored in worship, shrines, festivals, art, and literature. After Greece was Christianized, the old gods slipped into new forms. The patriarchal Olympic gods and even the older fertility goddesses live on in the hundreds of Christian saints. Demeter became Saint Dhimitra, and Artemis evolved into Saint Artemidus. Hera

metamorphosed into Saint Catherine, the saint of love and marriage. Poseidon transformed into Saint Nicholas. Today, sailors lash his icon on their masts and pray to him before making a journey.

This marble relief of a priest and priestess depicts amazonomachy, the term used to describe the wars between ancient Greeks and the Amazon women. Amazons were female warriors who lived on the outskirts of Greek society and were seen as brave, daring, and fearless. They worshiped Artemis, goddess of the hunt, and were primarily caretakers of animals. Amazon women fought only for territory. The Greeks and the Amazons coexisted peacefully until the Greeks coveted the prosperity of the Amazon society. War ensued, and the Amazons were exiled from their homeland.

ΑϹΑΤΕ ΤΩ ΙΚΩ ΑΙϹΜΑ ΚΑΙΝΟΝ· ΑϹΑΤΕ
ΤΩ ΙΚΩ ΠΑϹΑ Η ΓΗ·

ΑϹΑΤΕ ΤΩ ΙΚΩ ΕΥΛΟΓΗϹΑΤΕ ΤΟ ΟΝΟ
ΜΑ ΑΥΤΟΥ· ΕΥΑΓΓΕΛΙϹΑϹΘΑΙ ΗΜΕΡΑ
ΕΞ ΗΜΕΡΑϹ ΤΟ ϹΡΙΟΝ ΑΥΤΟΥ·

ΑΝΑΓΓΕΙΛΑΤΕ ΕΝ ΤΟΙϹ ΕΘΝΕϹΙΝ ΤΗ
ΔΟΞΑΝ ΑΥΤΟΥ· ΕΝ ΠΑϹΙΝ ΤΟΙϹ ΛΑ
ΟΙϹ ΤΑ ΘΑΥΜΑϹΙΑ ΑΥΤΟΥ·

ΟΤΙ ΜΕΓΑϹ ΚϹ ΚΑΙ ΑΙΝΕΤΟϹ ϹΦΟΔΡΑ
ΦΟΒΕΡΟϹ ΕϹΤΙΝ ΕΠΙ ΠΑΝΤΑϹ ΤΟΥϹ
ΘΕΟΥϹ·

ΟΤΙ ΠΑΝΤΕϹ ΟΙ ΘΕΟΙ ΤΩΝ ΕΘΝΩΝ
ΔΑΙΜΟΝΙΑ· Ο ΔΕ ΚϹ ΤΟΥϹ ΟΥΝΟΥϹ
ΕΠΟΙΗϹΕΝ·

ΕΞΟΜΟΛΟΓΗϹΙϹ ΚΑΙ ΩΡΑΙΟΤΗϹ ΕΝΩ
ΠΙΟΝ ΑΥΤΟΥ· ΑΓΙΟϹΥΝΗ ΚΑΙ ΜΕ
ΓΑΛΟΠΡΕΠΕΙΑ ΕΝ ΤΩ ΑΓΙΑϹΜΑ
ΤΙ ΑΥΤΟΥ·

ΕΝΕΓΚΑΤΕ ΤΩ ΙΚΩ ΑΙ ΠΑΤΡΙΑΙ ΤΩ
ΕΘΝΩΝ· ΕΝΕΓΚΑΤΕ ΤΩ ΙΚΩ ΔΟ
ΞΑΝ ΚΑΙ ΤΙΜΗΝ·

ΕΝΕΓΚΑΤΕ ΤΩ ΙΚΩ ΔΟΞΑΝ ΟΝΟΜΑ

THE ART AND ARCHITECTURE OF GREECE

7

For the ancient Greeks, art was a form of tribute or worship. Creating art was not just decoration or personal expression for the artist. The artists devoted themselves to their crafts and the study and mastery of skills. From the earliest times, Greek artists and architects were creating concepts of design, harmony, and proportion. The artists were more concerned with formal perfection than innovation, so development was gradual. Even everyday objects, like jars or pots, were crafted with great attention to materials and design.

The ultimate expression of Greek art and architecture was in the classical period. The Athenians believed that the perfection of form revealed the greatest expression of spirit. In the United States, the classical model of architecture is still alive in the Greek columns of the White House and almost every state capitol. The Lincoln Memorial was inspired by the colossal monuments of the Greek classical period.

Early Beginnings

The first great Greek sculpture came from the Bronze Age Cycladic civilization, between 3300 and 2000 BC. Many austere

This medieval Greek manuscript *(left)* depicts the construction of a church. While western European churches vaulted upward with tall spires and towers intending to reach heaven, Greek Orthodox churches brought heaven to earth with surrounding mosaics that created a sense of enclosure. The Queen's Megaron in the Palace of Minos *(above)* is a spacious suite of rooms with frescos decorating the walls. It has strong ties to Greek mythology with the Knossos floor plan used as its design for the labyrinth that contained the Minotaur in Greek mythology, and dates from 1700 BC.

The Room of the Blue Monkeys is part of a Minoan palace on the Aegean island of Thera, one of the islands that make up Santorini. The remnants of this fresco depict a family of blue monkeys climbing the island's volcano. The monkeys have a humanlike quality and were believed by the Minoans to be sacred animals that were servants to the gods.

geometric figures of white marble have been found, often at grave sites. Most of the figures are small female forms, though there are a few life-size statues. The marble was rubbed smooth by pebbles or emery, a granular mineral. These figures are similar to modern abstract sculptures.

The Minoans painted spectacular frescoes. Applying paint to wet plaster, the artists covered the walls with images of animals and scenes of dancing, games, and processions. Using bold colors, including reds, blues, greens, and yellows, they painted swirling shapes that suggested movement. This quality of energy and motion was unique to Minoan art. Their palaces were huge mazelike complexes. Built around a large courtyard, the palaces had hundreds of light-filled rooms.

The art of the Mycenaeans was influenced by that of the Minoans, and the Mycenaeans adopted Minoan painting techniques for use in their own frescoes. Their citadels were built with carefully fitted huge square blocks of stone. The structure of these fortresses, which had an open porch with columns to support the entrance, was similar to later classical architecture.

The Geometric and Orientalizing Periods

It is thought that geometric art originated in Athens. The Athenian artists were influenced by the geometric quality of the Cycladic figures. Initially, the designs of the geometric period, which lasted from 900 to 725 BC, were carefully organized semi-circles, zigzags, and other abstract forms. The early painting technique, called black-figure, was black paint applied on the reddish clay of the pot. Later, the artists added

This red-figure vase dates from the late geometric period (900–725 BC). It was during this time that the first animal and human figures were depicted, mostly in silhouette. Vases of this era expressed the ideology and values of the ruling class.

geometric figures of animals and humans. The human figures were sticklike, with tiny waists and large triangular thighs and shoulders. As the skills of the artists increased, they painted more complicated mythic scenes and stories on the pots. Geometric art, with its attention to form and composition, is the basis of all Greek art.

The next period, the orientalizing period, from approximately 725 through 630 BC, was influenced by forms and techniques from Anatolia, Egypt, and the Middle Eastern countries. The severe silhouettes of the geometric period expanded into more natural shapes. There were new animal shapes, real and fantastic, but still painted in geometric formal patterns. Figures were also still painted in black on the red background of the clay. Later the painting techniques were reversed. In the new red-figure painting, the vase was painted black and the figures were left in the red clay of the pot. The black-figure painting was done with a sharp point; the red-figure painting was done more subtly with a brush. This new brush technique enabled the artists to create more complicated scenes that suggested greater dimension and movement.

The Archaic and Classical Periods

In the new prosperity of the archaic period (650 to 480 BC), aristocrats and rich merchants hired sculptors to carve huge statues and carvings for grave markings.

Sculptors also created large statues of gods and humans. The male statues, *kouroi*, were always naked. The female figures, *korai*, were clothed in clinging tunics. Facing forward, often straight with clenched fists and stiff legs, the statues are Greek, but the wiglike hair is similar to the style of Egyptian art.

The Doric and the Ionic Order

The principal architectural orders were the Doric and Ionic. There was a third, the Corinthian, which evolved later. Doric columns rise from a plain platform and have twenty-four vertical grooves, known as flutes. Changing angles of sunlight and shadow play on the flutes to create a sense of dimension and motion. Doric columns are capped with a simple stone block called a capital.

Proportionally taller and slimmer, Ionic columns sit on a molded base. Their twenty-four flutes are each separated with a narrow band. The Ionic capital has ornate scrolls. The later Corinthian capitals were even more elaborately decorated.

Right below the roof, the top of the Doric temples had stone blocks called metopes. The metopes were separated by narrower rectangular stones called triglyphs. A frieze, a sculpted horizontal band around the temple, filled the metopes and triglyphs. The frieze was a form of bas-relief, in which sculpted figures were carved to project out of the flat stone. The Ionic frieze

The Temple of Athena Nike was built in 420 BC at the Acropolis. The temple was the first structure at the Acropolis to be built in the Ionic style, complete with four columns supporting each end of the temple.

was continuous, uninterruped by the metopes or triglyphs. There was a pediment, or a triangular gable, at either end of the temple. These pediments were often carved with scenes of mythology or history.

In the fifth century BC, the architects and sculptors freely mixed the Doric and Ionic orders. The Erechtheion, the Parthenon, and the other ruins on the Acropolis are stunning examples of their mastery.

Sulking Kore, a marble sculpture that dates to approximately 480 BC, is seen here. "Kore" means "maiden" in Greek, and refers to Persephone, the daughter of Demeter. Hades, god of the dead, kidnapped Persephone to be his wife. Demeter mourned the loss of her daughter and neglected her responsibilities as mother of the earth. As a result, the earth turned gray and barren. Zeus and Hades then agreed that Persephone would spend seven months in the living world with her mother and only five in the underworld.

By the seventh century BC, the essential elements of the later classical Greek architecture were in place. The early wooden temples had severe, vertically grooved columns of what came to be called the Doric order. The Doric order was a sturdy, simple, austere type of architecture. There was also a more decorated type of architecture called the Ionic order.

The art and architecture of the classical period (480–323 BC) were the perfect union of the early art and new knowledge. Classical forms absorbed the solidity of the Mycenaean citadels. They also had the strict form and composition of the geometric period (900–725 BC), which had its roots in the Cycladic art. Classical art also incorporated the free play of imagination, color, and sense of movement of the Minoans. With newly developed knowledge in mathematics, perspective, and building, the artists were able to shape stone with a new sense of texture, form, and movement.

The Caryatid Porch, part of the Erechtheion building located at Acropolis. Caryatids are columns designed to look like beautiful maidens and have both a decorative and structural function. They support the roof of the porch. The original caryatids were dismantled and are now housed at the Acropolis Museum. These are stone replicas.

Parthenon

Rising high on the Acropolis, the Parthenon can be seen from anywhere in Athens. Built to honor Athena, Athens's patron goddess, the Parthenon was also intended as a symbol of Athens's greatness. It is considered the greatest Doric temple ever built.

The centuries have been cruel to the Parthenon. Emperors, collectors, archaeologists, and vandals have carried off statues, carved pediments, and anything else they could. The Parthenon has been an Orthodox church, a mosque, and an ammunition storeroom. In the seventeenth century, gunpowder stored in the Parthenon was ignited. The explosion blew off the roof. The worst damage has come from the modern world. Pollution and acid rain have eaten away the golden outer shell of the marble, leaving it white and frail.

Among the remaining ruins, the Parthenon is still magnificent. Fifty huge marble columns rise against the azure backdrop of mountains, sea, and sky. The ancient architects refined the Doric principles of design and proportion. The columns are finer and taller, creating a sense of soaring grace. The columns are each slightly different but in complete harmony with each other. They gently swell from the base, giving a sense of rhythm and flowing movement. The perspective was manipulated with subtle curves and refinements. The solid and massive structure seems to float on the Acropolis. The Parthenon is a masterpiece of composition, perspective, and scale.

The architects built majestic public buildings and temples. In sculpture, there was a perfect blending of the ideal and real. The classical sculptures have a realistic loose-jointed fluidity and grace in their idealized stone forms. The work was created as a tribute to the gods and the community.

In 454 BC, Pericles masterminded a huge building project. The old wooden temples and buildings on the Acropolis had been destroyed by the Persians. New

marble buildings were to replace them. Pericles chose his friend, Phidias, the master sculptor, to direct the project. Hiring a team of the greatest architects, sculptors, and painters of the Greek world, Phidias created a spectacular complex of temples, buildings, arches, and sculptures.

Today, the little that remains of Phidias's creation is in ruins. The Propylaea, a monumental gateway, still stands. The ancient tomb and shrine, the Erechtheion, was restored in the 1980s. Among the ruins of the other buildings, the battered shell of the Parthenon is still magnificent.

The Acropolis Museum and other European museums house the remains of the pediments and bas-reliefs, or three-dimensional scenes carved into stone. One bas-relief, originally banding the top of the Parthenon, shows the carved history of Athens. A pediment, carved by Phidias, depicted the Panathenaea Festival, which was a festival dedicated to the goddess Athena. He carved young men on horses with bronze bridles, maidens, old men, and the citizens of Athens in ritual procession. Phidias also created a colossal

The 2,000-year old theater at Epidaurus, built by Polykleitos the Younger during the fourth century BC, is considered an architectural wonder for its semicircle construction hollowed out in the side of a hill. The inscribed names on its benches and thrones imply a relationship between the theater and the cult of Dionysus. Ancient Greeks considered it the most beautiful and harmonious theater in all of Greece. It is still in use from June to August when it is used for performances of Greek tragedies and comedies.

statue of Athena, almost 40 feet (12.2 m) high. Her face was ivory with jeweled eyes. Her tunic consisted of detachable solid gold bars, the treasury of Athens. This statue is gone. The rest of the Acropolis sculptures are in museums or were destroyed.

Theaters were temples to Dionysus. The first theater was built in the fifth century BC. Usually built into the side of a hill or mountain, theaters had a large raised stage called the orchestra. Rings of seats, rising from the orchestra, were carved into the rock. Besides being stunning, the Greek theaters had incredible acoustics. At Epidaurus, a 14,000-seat theater, a piece of paper can be torn in the orchestra and the sound can be heard in the last row. How the Greeks accomplished this is still not understood. Epidaurus, the theater at Delphi, the Herodes Atticus, and many other theaters are still used for performances of music and drama.

After the Peloponnesian War, Athens was ravaged. The city could no longer spon-

sor large projects. The great sculptor, Praxiteles, carved many new statues, but unfortunately, only a few works survived. In the work that did survive and even in later Roman copies, Praxiteles mastery of conception and carving can be experienced. His work had a new sensuality and elegance. The perfection of the finish on his human figures looks like real skin. It is thought that Praxiteles sculpted the first female nude, the Aphrodite of Cnidus.

Hellenic Period

In the Hellenic period, from 330 to 300 BC, Athens was flooded with immigrants from Alexander the Great's empire. Foreign artists brought new trends and techniques. They had incredible skills, but their work had no connection to political, religious, and spiritual life.

Working for wealthy patrons for the first time, the artists did portraits and used live models. No longer ideal, the work had a heaviness and lack of proportion. Art now showed life in all its forms with a wide range of emotions. Personal expression

This mosaic of the Pentecost *(left)* depicts the Madonna and child. There are nine rules that an artist typically follows when creating a religious icon. One states, "Never forget the joy of spreading icons in the world, the joy of icon painting, the joy of making a saint shine through the icon, and the joy of being in union with the saint being painted." *Coronation of the Virgin* by El Greco *(above)* dates from 1591. El Greco, born in Crete, lived his life in Toledo, Spain. He signed his paintings in Greek characters.

and fame were desired goals. For the first time, the work was valued for its artistic merit rather than for its meaning.

Rome and the Byzantine Empire

After 146 BC, Greece was a Roman province. Enamored with Greek art, the Romans carried off all they could. They commissioned Greek artists to make exact, lifeless copies of the great masterpieces. Intended for private art collections, art was for the pleasure and pride of rulers and wealthy men. However, by stealing and copying Greek art, the Romans preserved it.

In AD 330, Constantinople became the capital of the Roman Empire and the cultural center of the Byzantine Empire. The best Greek artists emigrated to Constantinople. They did their most beautiful work in the mosaics found there. Mosaics are pictures and designs made of bits of glass, stone, tile, and other materials set in mortar. The Byzantine mosaics, found in churches and public buildings, are spectacular. Artists created incredibly detailed scenes of mythology, saints, and Christian history with patterns of stone, glass, and sometimes even gold, silver, and jewels. Mosaic floors of pebbles and cockleshells can still be seen in homes throughout Greece.

Ottoman Empire

In 1453, the Turkish Ottoman Empire overthrew the Byzantine Empire. The Greek artists fled to Europe where they promoted their history, skills, and creativity. The Greek artists provided an invaluable source of inspiration and knowledge for the Renaissance. Originating in Italy, the Renaissance was the rediscovery and revival of art and literature based on the classical sources of the ancient world.

The Temple of Poseidon, located at Cape Sounion, sits on a platform overlooking the Aegean Sea and the surrounding islands. It was an ideal place for the ancient Greeks to worship their god of the sea. The temple originally had thirty-four marble columns built in the Doric style that could be seen by sailors miles away.

The floor plan and architectural elements seen in this illustration of the House of the Faun in Pompeii, Italy, depicts the various types of Greek columns utilized in its construction. This house combines both Italian and Hellenistic styles in the form of Italian sculpture and fountains and Greek mosaics and columns.

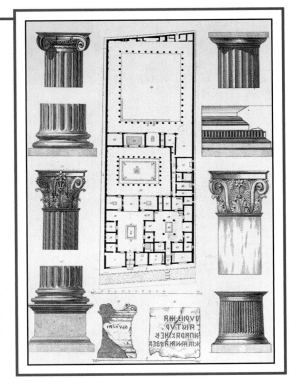

Under the oppressive rule of the Turks, the Greeks could only give their attention to the basic needs of survival. Painting still flourished on the Ionian Islands, though. Crete, free of Turkish rule until 1669, was home to a school of painting. The greatest Cretan painter, Domenicos Theotokopoulos, was known later as El Greco. Leaving Crete in his early twenties, he studied with the great Italian painters of the Renaissance. He spent the rest of his life in Spain. El Greco is known for his intensely emotional work, dramatic shading, and elongated figures.

Folk Art

The most remote mountain regions of Greece escaped the oppression of the Turks. There, folk art continued to flourish. Folk art did not require sponsorship by the state, the Church, or the wealthy. The women wove, knitted, and embroidered clothing, drapes, and furniture fabrics. Most homes had a hand loom. Geometric and oriental designs were and still are woven into wall hangings, pillowcases, and rugs. The men still carve Byzantine designs into wood furniture. This tradition of folk art has an unbroken lineage to the past.

Despite the thousands of treasures that still exist, very little ancient Greek art has survived. Except for pottery painting and the Minoan frescos, there is no painting. Most of the bronze statues were melted down centuries ago. The few that remain were discovered later in shipwrecks. Hundreds of statues have crumbled, and most of the temples have been reduced to rubble or are reconstructed ruins. However, museums in Greece and around the world house many great works of the past, and the spectacular ruins that remain in Greece continue to astound and inspire.

THE LITERATURE AND MUSIC OF GREECE

8

The ancient Greeks believed music, dance, and poetry were gifts of the gods. Though these arts were used for entertainment, they were an essential part of worship. Music, dance, and poetry were also considered essential for the development of body, mind, and spirit. To be educated was to be well versed in all these arts. In the ancient world, most men and women played at least one instrument and all Greeks danced. In their training, amateur and professional artists studied meter, form, and all the great works of the past.

Music

Only fragments of ancient music have survived, and it is not certain how music was performed. Musicians and their instruments are portrayed in statues, frescoes, and vase paintings. Some of the instruments were the *kithara*, a large lyre or harp; the *aulos*, a double-pipe reed instrument; and the *syrinx*, or panpipes. The Greeks also had many percussion instruments, including tambourines, cymbals, and a variety of drums.

These Greek women (*left*) perform a traditional folk dance. Each region has its own traditional dance and costume. Dancing is an important aspect of all celebrations throughout the country such as weddings, baptisms, name day (saint's day), and all religious holidays. A miniature painting on a wooden tablet (*above*) is dated 470 BC and depicts musicians in a sacrificial procession. This tablet is a rare specimen of Greek painting used for decorative purposes. All the participants wear garlands as two young boys play the kithara and flute.

The Greeks used modes, which are musical tones arranged in a scale. Different modes were thought to communicate specific feelings. The Dorian mode, thought to be solemn and martial, summoned courage. Thought to be wild and dissonant, the Phrygian mode inspired abandon. Much of the language and terminology of Western music came from the Greeks. Melody, harmony, and the names of the tones of a musical scale, like tonic or diatonic, are just some of the words and musical definitions that came from the ancient Greeks.

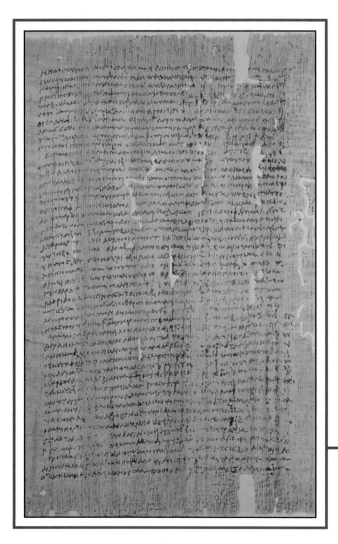

Dance

The ancient Greeks danced during festivals, processions, funerals, and weddings. Dance was used for physical and military training. After a victory, a general might dance instead of giving a speech. In some festivals and competitions, women were allowed to dance. This was their only opportunity to publicly display their beauty and grace.

The Minoan frescoes depicted variations of the circle dance, which was believed to have a magical and purifying effect. In this dance, men and women circled a sacred object, possibly an altar or a tree. The Minoans had a maze dance in which dancers moved in winding patterns. There were animal

The Athenian Constitution was written by Aristotle in 350 BC. This is the only surviving manuscript, which was inscribed in an Egyptian papyrus book. The Constitution has two parts. Part one recounts the history of the Athenian government, the original constitution, and the eleven changes to the original. Part two describes the operation of the government and the laws governing the city at the time of Aristotle.

dances to invoke the gods and hypnotize prey. At the symposiums, the elaborate dinner feasts held by and for Greek men, dancers performed for entertainment.

Modern choreographers have been inspired by the ancient dances. Isadora Duncan found inspiration in the poses of the painted dancers and in the flow and movement of Greek architecture. Duncan and Martha Graham were inspired by the dramatic folds and flowing fabrics of the dancers' clothing as seen in Greek frescoes and sculpture. Contemporary choreographers, such as American Mark Morris, have re-created the simple patterns of the Greeks' ritual dances.

Ancient Poets

Ancient music and poetry were aspects of the same art. Composed or improvised, poems were literally sung. Lyric poetry was sung to music played on a lyre. Homer is considered the father of Greek literature. Strumming or plucking a lyre, he told stories using the epic form, the narration of heroic deeds in elevated verse. The verse followed strict metric rules. The aristocrat Pindar (c. 518–438 BC) was known for his eloquence and metrical complexity. Almost all of his forty-four surviving poems are

This marble relief depicts Homer with Clio, the Muse of history, on the side of the Sarcophagus of the Muses. Homer is believed to have lived during the ninth or eighth century BC. He is credited with composing *The Iliad* and *The Odyssey*, which are considered two of the oldest epic poems in Western civilization.

Depicted here is a marble bust of Aeschylus, the father of Greek drama. Aeschylus's tragedies are the first known plays in existence. During his life he produced, designed, and acted in his plays. He is credited with adding a second character to the stage called an antagonist and is considered the father of tragedy.

odes in honor of victories at war or athletic games. "Ode" comes from the Greek *oide*, meaning "song." Born on the island of Lesbos, Sappho (early sixth century BC) is considered the finest woman poet of the ancients. Many critics consider her among the finest poets of either sex. An aristocrat, she was educated and ran a school for girls. Only fragments of her poetry, love lyrics, and hymns have survived.

Drama and the Playwrights

Drama evolved from the springtime worship of Dionysus. The early festivals were celebrated with dancing, singing, and the sacrifice of a goat. Tragedy, a kind of drama, comes from the Greek *tragoidia*, meaning "goat's song." A dancer would tell the entire story of a myth through movement. Accompanied by the shrill, piercing aulos, a chorus would sing a wild, emotional hymn called a *dithyramb*.

By the fifth century BC, the Athenian Festival of Dionysus was a publicly funded civic and sacred

Sophocles, the greatest of the Greek playwrights, won first prize at his first competition at the Theater of Dionysus, defeating Aeschylus. Sophocles had an innovative approach to playwriting. He was the first playwright to write plays not in the form of a trilogy, which was common, but to condense all the action into one play, making the tragedy an entity in itself. Sophocles is also credited with the invention of scene painting.

Euripides, an unsuccessful playwright during his lifetime, posthumously achieved fame as a tragic poet. Aristotle regarded his plays, many of which dealt with personal issues, as models for other tragedies. Euripides brought the common man to the stage by showing Greece's heroes as regular men.

event. The Athenians spent more money on dramatic festivals than on their military budget. Over the centuries, the Dionysian ritual had expanded. A longer story, actors, scenic elements, costumes, and a more extensive musical score were gradually added. People traveled great distances to see the plays. Women were not allowed to perform, and it is still not certain if they were allowed to attend these events. Beginning in the morning, three tragedies and a comedy were performed. A comic interlude, called a satyr play, followed each tragedy. A prize of money was awarded to the best playwright of the day.

Written in the classical period, the plays of the three great tragedians, Aeschylus, Sophocles, and Euripides, are equal to the greatest dramas ever written. They all used the plots and characters of Greek mythology for their tragedies. However, they handled their material very differently, which reflected the political, spiritual, and psychological changes in the society. The playwrights also acted, directed, danced, designed sets and costumes, and wrote the music. Each one brought new innovations to the theater. Being a theatrical artist was not a profession. The great tragedians were also soldiers, statesmen, and public officials.

This eighth-century BC bronze ritual *tympanon* (drum) depicts Zeus mounted on a bull and flanked by two corybantes, his protectors. About fifty pieces of music survive from ancient Greece. Instruments were mainly used as accompaniment since importance was placed on the singer's voice.

Aeschylus, who lived between 525 and 456 BC, wrote around ninety tragedies of which only seven have survived. Celebrated for his grand and rugged style, he won thirteen first prizes during the Dionysian festivals. His *Prometheus Unbound* is considered the first great surviving tragedy. Sophocles, who lived between 496 and 406 BC, was loved for his simple, lucid, and elegant writing. He won first prize at least twenty times. Only seven tragedies have survived from the 127 that he wrote. Among them are the great *Antigone* and *Oedipus at Colonus*. Euripides wrote some seventy-five plays before his death in 406 BC, of which eighteen have survived. His work was considered very controversial, and he won only five first prizes. His work was very dark, disturbing, and modern. In the late 1960s, the junta banned productions of his plays, which include *Electra*, *The Cyclops*, *Medea*, *Orestes*, and many more.

Aristophanes, who lived from 450 to around 388 BC, was the greatest Greek comedic writer. He wrote at least fifty-four comedies, of which eleven have survived. No one was safe from his scathing satire. Brutal to politicians, Aristophanes also poked fun at his fellow playwrights. *The Frogs*, *The Clouds*, and perhaps the first antiwar play, *Lysistrata*, are still often produced in theaters around the world.

Byzantine Music and Poetry

During the centuries of unrest and poverty, Greek artists migrated to find work. After Constantinople became the capital of the Roman Empire, Greek musicians and poets settled there. Influenced by the music of Jewish synagogue services, Greek musicians developed the Byzantine church chant. Poets and musicians also wrote court music for special occasions and to win favor with the emperor.

When Constantinople fell to the Turks, the Greek musicians and poets escaped to other parts of Europe. Along with other Greek artists and scholars, they influenced the Renaissance. Poetry flourished on Crete until the island fell to the Turks. Escaping to the Ionian Islands, the Cretan poets continued to develop but were isolated from the rest of Greece. Except for the music of Orthodox Church services, Greek music, dance, and poetry stayed alive in folk forms.

Folk Songs and Dances

To escape the Turks, some Greeks left their villages to join roving mountain bands. Called *klephts* by the Turks, the bands had their own minstrels. They composed songs telling of heroic deeds and the struggle for freedom. From other regions, folk songs tell of the need for love and the enjoyment of simple pleasures. Mourning

songs, sung by professional mourners, accented each line of the song with wails and shrieks. Some of the most expressive songs come from the fierce Mani people of the Peloponnese.

Many of the ancient folk dances have survived. The sword dance, mentioned by Homer, is still performed in Crete. Each region has its own dances, though some are known and performed throughout Greece. From the Peloponnese, the *kalamatiano* is considered the national dance of Greece. In a line, dancers hold each other's hands with their elbows bent at right angles. The leader dances intricate variations of the main steps. From Epirus, the *tsamiko* was the favorite dance of the mountain fighters in World War II. In this dance, women stand in a line, and they dance simple steps. They wear the traditional costume with a velvet bodice, white stockings, and a yellow-and-blue-striped apron over a full skirt. Part of the skirt is folded back to reveal a red lining. At the peak of the dance, the male leader performs acrobatic leaps and whirls, slapping both heels in midair and striking the ground with the palm of his hand. Often performed

Greek dancing is often categorized by two distinct styles: shuffling and leaping. However, every dance in Greece has specific regional characteristics. Generally, the shuffling dances are performed in the plains, while leaping dances occur in the mountains. Dances that originated from mainland Greece tend to be slow and heavy-footed. In Cyclades, dances involving pairs are popular: men dancing with men, women dancing with women, and men dancing with women.

spontaneously in *tavernas*, the *zeibekiko* is sometimes called the dance of the eagle. It is an ancient dance of combat. Stretching out his arms like wings of a bird, the dancer circles around his partner or if he is alone, his imaginary antagonist. Eyes cast down, he moves as if in a trance, sometimes hissing like a bird of prey. There are hundreds of folk dances. Greek folk dancing troupes perform their dances throughout the world.

Independence

After being silenced for the four hundred years of Ottoman rule, Greek writers searched for a new voice and language. They struggled to reconnect to the past and to explore what it meant to be Greek in this new world. In the tradition of their ancestors, modern Greek poets and writers were also soldiers, statesmen, public servants, and patriots. In their individual ways, they explored classical ideas of rhythm, balance, and proportion. Blending common speech, folk songs, and the past, Dionysios Solomós, who lived from 1798 to 1857, forged the path for the writers who followed.

Odysseus Elytis (pseudonym Odysseus Alepoudhelis, 1911–1996) won the Nobel Prize in literature in 1979. He was the most prominent Greek poet dedicated to the resistance and struggle for freedom. Elytis formed many of his stylistic techniques from his associations with avant-garde figures such as Pablo Picasso, Henri Matisse, André Breton, and Marc Chagall. His work focused on creating a new literary style for modern Greece.

C. P. Cavafy lived from 1863 to 1933 in the Greek community in Alexandria. His poetry explored what it meant to be a Hellene, as well as the relationship of the distant past with the present. Kostís Palamás (1859–1943) saw the literatures of the world as an interconnected whole. In his *Poems Out of Season*, he wrote, "I am a citizen of the world / And the earth is my fatherland." At Palamás's funeral, crowds of mourners defiantly sang Solomós's "Hymn to Freedom," Greek's national anthem, in front of the German occupiers.

The first Greek to be awarded the Nobel Prize for literature, Giorgos Seferis explored themes of alienation, wandering, and Hellenism. He lived from 1900 to 1971. Inspired by Homer, he used *The Iliad* and *The Odyssey* as sources for his work *Mythistorema*. Born on Crete in 1911, Odysseus Elytis was awarded the Nobel Prize for literature in 1979. His poems weave in phrases from Homer, Sappho, Orthodox Church service, folk songs, and scholarly references. When Elytis died in 1996, all of Greece went into mourning.

Modern Music

Greek composers also struggled for a new voice. Looking to the European musical tradition, some Greek composers copied foreign forms. Other composers looked to Greek folk music for inspiration. *Rebetika* came from Eastern rhythms of Turkey, Byzantine hymns, and folk songs. Similar to American jazz in origin, rebetika came from the lower levels of society, such as the docks, slums, and opium dens. The Greeks heard the beauty of the music and changed the grim stories to songs of hopes and dreams.

Modern Greek composers have synthesized twentieth-century European harmonic developments with the unusual rhythms, plaintive sounds, and instruments of Greek folk music. Manos Hadjidakis won an Oscar for his bouzouki score of the film *Never on Sunday* (1960). Considered Greece's greatest living composer, Mikis Theodorakis has written many scores. He has also written for films, among them, *Zorba the Greek* and *Serpico*. Other important composers are Nikos Skalkottas, Manolis Kalomiris, and Yannis Xenakis.

Renowned Greek composer Mikis Theodorakis composed music based on Greek poetry and is recognized as a musician of genius. In 1967, a Fascist junta rose to power, and he was forced underground. Afterwards, the army banned people from playing and listening to his music. Theodorakis, who fought for the return of democracy to Greece, gave more than a thousand worldwide concerts for the cause.

Music, dance, and poetry sustain the Greeks like air. There have been hundreds of great Greek musicians and poets, and it cannot be stressed enough all that these artists have contributed to their country. Most of them were soldiers who fought and were injured and tortured. They also served as statesmen who gave their energies to nurture their country and fellow citizens. Musicians and poets were and still are the channel for the thoughts, feelings, and history of their compatriots.

FAMOUS FOODS AND RECIPES OF GREECE

9

T he ancient Greeks considered cooking an art. From a simple country meal to a lavish banquet, to the Greeks eating has always been for the body, the senses, and the soul. A Greek wrote the first cookbook around 350 BC. In the second century AD, Athenaeus wrote his fifteen-volume *Deipnosophistae*, "The Philosophy of Dining." The surviving volumes are full of details about food preparation, presentation, health benefits, and feasts. In ancient times, a Greek cook was a prize. Wealthy Macedonians, Romans, and Byzantines all wanted Greek cooks.

Ancient Greek cooking influenced the entire Mediterranean world. Bouillabaisse, a French fish stew, was created by Greeks who settled the Marseilles area in the sixth century BC. *Skordalia*, a garlic-flavored mayonnaise, became the French *aioli*. Many herbs, polenta, dumplings, and gingerbread all came from the early Greeks. To escape slavery, some Greek cooks sought refuge in monasteries. They wore the monk's black robes but had on a billowy white hat instead of the black hat of the monks. This is the same hat master chefs wear today.

The Greeks eat as they have for centuries. They enjoy simple, flavorful, nutritious food that is meant to be shared with others. They know the artful use of herbs

A Greek family *(left)* enjoys dinner together. Greeks commonly enjoy a Mediterranean diet consisting of fish, olive oil, lemons, tomatoes, and herbs. This way of eating is considered healthy because red meat is consumed sparingly, and olive oil and fish do not have the same cholesterol-raising effects as foods high in saturated fats. Greeks begin their meals with *mezédes*, a variety of appetizers. The most popular is *taramosaláta*, a dip made of fish roe. An appetizer called *dolmadakia (above)*, is comprised of meat, rice, and onions wrapped with large grape leaves.

Main courses at a Greek meal may be a casserole, fish, or lamb, the favored meat in Greece. A popular Greek entrée is *moussaká*, layers of eggplant and meat baked in a tangy sauce. It is said that there are four secrets to Greek cuisine: fresh ingredients, the liberal use of herbs and spices, olive oil, and simplicity. The most important of these is the olive oil, present in just about every Greek dish. The Greeks' long life expectancy is attributed to olive oil since it has been proven to lower cholesterol.

and vegetables to subtly flavor meat, fish, grains, and beans. Recipes have been passed down for generations with each island or family adding a special little twist. Country and island women harvest wild capers, herbs, nuts, and fruits. Mothers pass on the knowledge of wild greens to their daughters.

Greeks value fresh foods as well. Greens just harvested from the earth and octopus just caught from the sea are to be savored. Nothing is wasted. The olive mash left after pressing the olives for oil is used for fertilizer. *Dolmas* are tender grape leaves stuffed with seasoned rice or grain and possibly bits of meat. Tough grape leaves wrap roasts or meat for grilling. Greek food is served leisurely and attractively, in beautiful surroundings with family and friends.

In the country and on the islands, food has escaped the blandness of industrialization. Villagers and islanders have gardens. Even city-dwellers often have little roof gardens. The goats graze on mountain grasses and herbs. Their meat, milk, and cheese have a unique and subtle flavor not to be found in mass-produced food. Honey is another favorite food, so many Greeks keep beehives. The island winds are thought to blow away impurities, leaving unspoiled flowers and herbs for the bees. There is thyme-infused honey from the bees that feed on wild thyme. There is also eucalyptus honey, lemon blossom honey, rosemary honey, and so on.

Today, the Mediterranean diet is recommended for health reasons. In the 1950s, a study was done on the diet of the people of Crete. They had less obesity, increased longevity, and lower rates of cancer and cardiovascular disease. It was determined that their low-fat, mostly vegetable diet was the reason for their good health.

Meals

A Greek breakfast is generally a light one and might include fresh fruit, sheep's milk yogurt with honey, cheese, bread, and coffee. The fruit, figs, or grapes can be wild or cultivated. Cheese is often goat's milk feta, which has a mild, tangy, and slightly salty taste, or pure white ewe's milk *kasseri*. The Greeks love coffee, particularly the very strong, sweetened coffee that first came from the Turks.

Dinner and lunch food is similar. In the country, lunch is the main meal and dinner is light. In the city, lunch is light and dinner is late and leisurely. Most Greeks still take a siesta after lunch. From 2:30 to 4:30, particularly in the summer, shades are drawn and life comes to halt.

Light traditional Mediterranean fare such as this is often accompanied by alcohol. Not merely meant to satisfy the appetite, these small meals combine eating with socializing, a common pastime in Greece.

Tzatziki

Four servings
1 large cucumber, peeled, minced
  or grated, and drained
2 cups yogurt*
1–3 garlic cloves or 4 green onions.
  Cloves, crushed through a garlic press
Salt and pepper

Combine all ingredients in a glass bowl.
Mix well and refrigerate. Serve cold with
pita bread or vegetables.

*Buy the richest yogurt available. Line a sieve
with cheesecloth and allow yogurt to drain
overnight at room temperature before preparing.*

Dinner always begins with a leisurely sampling of *mezédes*, the Greek word for appetizers. There are cheeses, olives, and *dolmas*. There are dips for vegetables, such as *tzatziki*, a yogurt-cucumber mixture, and *taramasalata*, creamy fish roe. From the sea come squid, octopus, sea urchins, and lobster. Meat mezédes might be sausages or spiced meat wrapped in phyllo. Wine and ouzo, the Greek national drink, are sipped. Ouzo is the distilled residue of pressed grapes flavored with aniseed.

Soup is served for dinner or as the main dish for lunch. Since ancient times, the Greeks have made lentil soups and *fassolada*, a hearty bean soup served with crushed onions. Bean soups are eaten during Lent when meat, fish, and dairy are forbidden. *Avgolemono* is a golden lemony soup that is also used as a sauce.

To break the Lent fast, there is a special Easter soup. The entrails of the Easter lamb are used to make a broth. It is seasoned with scallions and dill, and at the last moment, avgolemono sauce is added.

Dinner includes many vegetables. There are *yigendes*, which are large lima beans in tomato sauce, or greens prepared in many different ways. Fish, always fresh, is cooked simply with herbs and olive oil. Squid and cuttlefish can be eaten during Lent since these fish do not have red blood. Greeks also love to eat all the wild birds, such as partridges, pheasants, and doves. Birds can be stuffed with rice, pine nuts, currants, or chestnuts. Meat is eaten sparingly. For special occasions like Easter, lamb is the favorite.

The Greeks also love sweets. Cakes are often taken with coffee in the early evenings before dinner. There are special breads and cakes for holidays and festivals. *Epitaphios*, a special Easter bread, is made with basil, sprinkled with holy water, and decorated with flowers.

Since antiquity, the Greeks have cultivated the grape, and they have made many brandies and wines. From the island of Skyros, there is a sour cherry brandy, spiced with cinnamon and orange. There are many fine red, white, and rosé wines. The most distinctive wine is ancient humble *retsina*. It is a white wine with the distinct taste of turpentine. Some say the taste of retsina came from the resin that lined ancient wine jars. The resin from pine trees prevented the jars from sweating and spoiling the wine. Another theory is that the early Greeks put pine tar in the wine jars to make their wine distasteful to the invading Persians. The Persians found the wine undrinkable, but the Greeks liked the taste.

Greeks only drink alcoholic drinks with food. The wine enhances the food and is used for toasting. Clear wineglasses are always clinked. This is a tradition representing the Greek belief that wine should be savored with all senses. The bouquet is for the nose, the color for the eyes, the flavor for taste, and the clinking for the ears. A guest will raise his glass to toast the hostess, saying, *"Yassou,"* meaning "Your health." Then he will spill a few drops of wine on the ground so the ancestors can also drink.

Marinated Feta with Greek Olives

2 roasted red bell peppers
1 lb. feta cheese, cut into cubes
1 cup fresh black Greek olives, pitted
½ cup olive oil
1 small red onion, chopped
2 teaspoons minced garlic
2 teaspoons fresh thyme
Salt and freshly ground pepper
1 tablespoon balsamic vinegar
Lemon juice to taste

Combine the peppers, feta, and olives in a large bowl. Add the olive oil and toss gently. Add the remaining ingredients and toss gently again. Adjust seasonings to taste; cover and chill at least five hours before serving. Serve with toasted pita.

DAILY LIFE AND CUSTOMS IN GREECE

10

The family is the center of daily life. Families are smaller than in the past, but the roots are long and deep through the extended family and community. Couples have an average of two children. Children stay in close contact with their cousins. They are all part of a *parea*, a tightly knit group of friends who go through life together. When a couple marries, the woman becomes part of her husband's parea, and he becomes part of hers.

A recent UNICEF study on European and central Asian children, ages nine through seventeen, found that Greek children were by far the happiest and most optimistic. The children said they trusted their parents and felt they could talk with them. According to the study, Greek children value personal relationships and have highly developed social consciences. The study concluded that the strength of the family was the reason for such positive findings.

Children

Almost always, the eldest son is named after his paternal grandfather and the eldest daughter after her paternal grandmother. However, on the Aegean Islands, girls are named after the maternal grandmother. The younger children are usually named after saints.

Grandparents play with their grandchild *(left)* in the Jewish Martyrs Quarter on the island of Rhodes. Like other cultures do, the Greeks celebrate their extended families and often include grandparents, aunts, uncles, and cousins in family events. While in the past Greek families tended to be large with many children, the average family size in Greece is decreasing. This is partly due to the increase of women in the workforce who have a lack of child care options and a shift of families moving to cities from rural areas. Family members in this photograph *(above)* pose outside a home on the island of Rhodes.

This is a view of a street in the old Plaka district of Athens, which is situated at the foot of the Acropolis. The area is referred to as the "neighborhood of the gods." During Turkey's control of Greece, Athens was comprised of only a little more than the Plaka district. Today, many of the streets are closed to automobile traffic and amplified music has been outlawed in order to retain the neighborhood's quaint atmosphere. The district's buildings have also been restored, making it a popular attraction for tourists and Greeks alike.

Children are never named for their parents. Nonreligious families often name their children after ancient figures like Aristotle or the goddess Aphrodite.

A Greek child has his or her parents and godparents to care for him or her. To be a godfather is a sacred duty and the godfather is tied not only to the godchild, but to his or her entire family. It is more binding than blood, because to accept the honor of godfather is a personal choice.

Greek children are carefully dressed when they go outside of the home, and they are very polite. Elders are addressed with a title, *Kyrie* for "Mister" or *Thie* for "Uncle." Children generally live at home until they are married. A young man might rent an apartment with a group of friends, but he will often come home to eat and sleep.

Greeks are very generous. In southern Greece and on the islands, when daughters marry, they receive furniture, houses, or money. In northern regions, the bride goes to live with her in-laws. Sons get financial support when they begin their careers.

Children ask for the blessing of their parents for any major endeavor, like marriage or a new job. Disrespect is dangerous and harmful. A parent's curse is powerful. It is thought that if God hears the curse, he will take his protection away from the child.

Fathers and Mothers

Fathers work reasonable hours so they can spend time with their families. They work to have a life; life is not sacrificed to work. Most Greek businesses would not think of transplanting a family man to another city or country since the family has deep roots and support in the community. In most families, the father is responsible for discipline. The mother does everything else. She cooks, cleans, shops, and serves the children and her husband. Despite the feminist movement, change for women in Greece has been slow. As in many countries, modern women have a job during the day and all the family chores at night.

On some of the Aegean Islands, women are the center of family life. Traditionally, the men have been sailors or worked abroad. The women had to handle the family business. On some islands, women own the land and the house, and the mother's fortune goes to the firstborn daughter.

Philitimo, Philoxenia and *Patrida*

The Greeks have three sacred, ancient values or traditions that they try to instill in their children. The Greek word *philitimo*, in which *philo* means "loving," and *timi* means "honor," is

Greeks have strong ties to their native village, district, or province. When Greeks meet one another, they often ask each other what region they are from in order to determine if they originated from the same area or have relatives there. This exchange allows Greeks to create a kinship with non-relatives while they are away from home.

Many of the towns and cities in modern Greece retain their ancient roots in an urban environment. Cars, buses, and taxis maneuver through the narrow, winding streets that date from ancient times. Shops and restaurants inhabit the same area as historical monuments. This is exemplified in Athens where the Acropolis dominates the landscape of this now urban city.

generally translated as self-esteem, but the meaning of the word is more complicated. It is an inner sense of individuality, dignity, and freedom. A person of philitimo is courteous and generous to all. It also means one is demanding and deserving of respect. A person of philitimo would never disgrace his family.

Philoxenia is the sacred duty of hospitality. It means respect for the needs of guests and strangers, and the sacred obligation to fulfill those needs. In ancient times, traveling was difficult and often perilous. People needed to depend and rely on each other.

Patrida, meaning "fatherland," refers to the loyalties and interdependence of not just the family, but of all Greek people. In the harsh life of the past, no one could survive alone. Life was not possible without cooperation and caring for others. The first loyalties extend to the family. The parents devote themselves to raising the children. It is a child's duty to share his home with his parents as long as they live. Elderly people are respected and have a function in the family.

These three ancient, sacred values are the backbone of the Greek character, family, and community. Greece has one of the lowest crime rates in the world. There is far less terrorism, violent crime, robbery, and domestic violence in Greece than in any other European country. Family disappointment and shame are much greater constraints than jail.

These sacred traditions have sustained the Greek people through the bleakest times of their history. Reduced to virtual slavery under the Turks, they preserved their sense of dignity and inner freedom. During World War II and the civil wars, the Greeks suffered

through incredible hardships and deprivation. Still, they would give their last blanket to a soldier. They would offer their roofless, bombed-out home as shelter to a stranger. Philitimo, philoxenia, and patrida define what it is to be Greek.

Talking and Meeting Places

Greeks have always loved to talk. Conversation is a national pastime. In the country, the village square is the meeting place. Children run off to skateboard or play soccer. At the village spring, the women fill their water jugs and talk. The men gather in coffee shops and talk. In the cities, men and women meet at coffee shops or tavernas. Fingering worry beads and drinking endless cups of coffee, they talk. On the islands, when the weather is bad, the men sit out the storm and talk. The women meet at the market or congregate at the village bakery. Dramatic, opinionated, and curious, the Greeks passionately discuss their families, art, philosophy, politics, and world affairs.

Because Greeks value personal contact, socializing is a popular activity. They enjoy talking about sports (especially the Olympics), food, wine, and Greece's contributions to history. Greeks generally shake hands firmly and make direct eye contact when meeting and departing. Men also may slap a friend's shoulder. Family members embrace and kiss.

EDUCATION AND WORK IN GREECE

11

Since ancient times, education has been very important to the Greeks. After independence, Greece became the first European country to have free compulsory education for children. Almost all Greek children complete their required schooling. Greece and Italy have the highest percentage of nonworking children in Europe. With free education and great value placed on learning, Greece has a very high literacy rate.

Compulsory education begins at age six and continues for nine years. At first level, children ages four through six attend kindergarten. The first two years are optional. After kindergarten, they attend elementary school until they are twelve. The second level or secondary school begins with three years at the *gymnasium*, or high school. Students have the option to go on to the *lyceum*. All education and textbooks are free. High school students can choose schools specializing in different areas, such as literature, science, history, language, sports, or the arts. There are also vocational

schools specializing in training people for agricultural, commercial, or technical work. The government does not provide any funding for private schools; still, some wealthy

A silversmith *(left)* works in Greece's Epirus region. During the Ottoman years, this area developed as an artistic center for goldsmiths and silversmiths, and the workmanship of its local artisans is still renowned throughout the country. Greek jewelry manufacturers do not utilize modern equipment, preferring instead to rely on their skills as craftsmen who are aware of Greece's long tradition of metalworking. School children *(above)* stand in front of the Parthenon in Athens. According to the Greek government, the goal of secondary education is to develop well-rounded, intellectual citizens with complete personalities who can live creatively, regardless of gender.

families send their children to private schools or abroad for their education. The academic year begins in the second half of September and ends in the second week of June.

Greece has twenty public universities with extensions throughout the country. The government forbids private universities. There are also foreign university branches. University education and textbooks are free for Greek citizens. For poorer students there are scholarships for food and transportation. There is also aid for political refugees and continuing education for adults.

Founded in the early nineteenth century, the National Technical University of Athens and the Aristotle University of Thessaloníki are the oldest and most prestigious schools. Because Greece has so few universities, there is stiff competition for acceptance. Students must take difficult entrance exams. Some students take special courses during their high school years to prepare for the university entrance exams.

Greek men, from eighteen to fifty years old, may be called for military service. There is compulsory military service for twenty to twenty-four months for young men. Women may serve only in select branches of the military. The minister of defense recently ordered thousands of books to be sent to troops serving at the northern borders. The books reflect Greek reading habits. Their subjects include mostly literature, prose and poetry, fine art, the sciences, history, geography, and a small selection of best-sellers. To relieve the stress of military life, the defense ministry is providing Internet cafés, lending libraries, and concerts.

The School Day

On a typical school day, students are picked up by the bus around 8 AM. In the morning hours, they attend classes. All

The primary school students in this photograph are eager to answer a question. It is traditional in many Greek schools to begin the school year with a benediction by a priest who blesses the students with a sprig of basil dipped in holy water. The Greek government mandated that religious education is compulsory for all Greek Orthodox students.

Greek gymnasium students, ages twelve through fourteen, study the same curriculum. They study classic Greek literature, modern Greek, math, physics, and chemistry. They also have courses in art, computer science, foreign languages, and religion. They take exams throughout the year to determine if they are ready to move on to more advanced courses. After morning classes, they have a break for a snack and activities outside. They have afternoon classes and then return home around 3:30 PM. At night, mothers help their children with homework until bedtime.

Students touring the National Archaeological Museum in Athens look at a bronze statue known as *The Jockey of Artemision*. Many schools with relatively easy access to museums use field trips to teach about Greek culture and heritage.

During the school year, classes are suspended for religious and national holidays. The summer break can last from one to two months, but some children attend summer school. In their free time, Greek children like to skateboard and play soccer, basketball, and volleyball. They visit museums and ruins. They also put on plays and concerts for family and friends. Urban children have video games and CD players. Country children have fewer modern games, and they have less free time because they must help out with farming chores.

Olympiad

In Greek classrooms, students learn the history of the ancient Olympics, which was held from 776 BC to AD 395. They read ancient authors' accounts of the games. They also study Pindar's odes that celebrate Olympic victories. The children study the modern Olympics that began in 1896. They discuss the meaning of the Olympic Creed, which was written for the modern games. It states: "The most important thing in the Olympic Games is not to win but to take part, just as the most important thing in life is not the triumph but the struggle."

Students train in the Olympic sports. They run footraces, jump, and throw the javelin and discus. They also box and wrestle. They track the route of the ancient marathon runner, the same route that will be used for the marathon in the 2004 Olympics.

At Olympia, the site of the ancient Olympics, students can walk through an arch to ruins of Zeus's temple. They can see the track where ancient chariot drivers raced their teams of horses. At the site's museum, they can see the great art from the original temple.

Students are participating in the international Cultural Olympiad. This is the government-sponsored arts festival currently being held throughout Greece. They attend performances and exhibits.

Through the Olympiad program, students are learning about their unique history and Greece's legacy to the world. They will be the informed hosts and guides for the millions of visitors attending the 2004 Athens Olympics.

Government Goals and Special Programs

Greek children are far behind the rest of Europe in their knowledge of computer technology. The government is making a great effort to provide computers and Internet access for both students and teachers. Already, most secondary schools are online, but elementary schools lag far behind. Many libraries are online. The government also is increasing funds for programs to serve children with learning disabilities. It is trying to mainstream children with special needs as much as possible. This means it tries to keep these children in regular classes as much as possible.

The Greek Ministry of Education and the 2004 Olympic Organizing Committee have joined forces to create the Olympiad. This is a learning program about the Olympics for elementary and high school students throughout Greece. Once a week, students have classroom study, practice Olympic sports, or take field trips to archaeological sites and museums. Through their study of the ancient games, students learn about art, history, archaeology, mythology, and philosophy. They also learn about the true meaning of the Olympic ideals and spirit.

Work

After World War II, many Greeks moved to the cities. Now, two-thirds of the Greek people live in urban areas. Greek city life and work are similar to city life and work around the world. Greeks work in factories, tanneries, refineries, banking, clerical jobs, and in advertising and government positions. There are about a dozen private sector unions and two public sector unions. The public unions are well organized and very powerful.

Being independent, most Greeks prefer to own and run their own businesses. Most businesses are small, with ten or fewer employees. Greeks prefer to buy from small stores, and neighborhoods are full of small shops. There are butchers, bakers, and grocers. The entire family shares the work in small shops. In restaurants, even small children will wait on customers or clear dishes.

For shop owners and city office workers, the day begins around 8 AM. Shops are open Monday through Saturday. Many businesses still shut down at 1:30 PM for the afternoon siesta. Around 5 PM, shops reopen and workers return. They end the day around 8:30 PM. For commuters, the afternoon siesta means they have to drive through four rush hours. The siesta is a cherished tradition, particularly in the

Many Greeks such as this shopkeeper work in the morning, rest in the afternoon when the heat is the strongest, and return to work at dusk. Workers are paid their regular monthly salary plus bonuses equivalent to a month's salary for Christmas, a half-month's salary for Easter, and another half-month's salary as a vacation allowance.

warmer months. Only international businesses keep a nine-to-five day all year.

Despite the women's movement of the 1980s, professional life for Greek women has been slow to change. In 1952, women were finally able to vote and hold elected office. However, women are less represented in the Greek government than elsewhere in Europe. Women are often paid less than men for the same work. They also are usually assigned jobs with less responsibility and authority. However, women are slowly entering the professional fields and government.

Many Greek islanders still depend on the land and sea for their livelihood. There are sailors, fishermen, farmers, and the tourist industry. Greek ship owners control the largest merchant fleet in the world, which is almost equal those of to all of the commonwealth nations combined. Most fishermen have small boats. Due to overfishing, they must travel far to get their catch. This has caused many islands to develop fish farming. Eating fish has become a luxury for most Greeks. Most of the catch is for

The raising of sheep and goats for wool, meat, and dairy products is a major economic industry in Greece. Both sheep milk and goat milk are used in the production of many cheeses, which are a popular export.

Athenian restaurants and island restaurants catering to tourists.

Farms tend to be small. Many families have at least 5 to 10 acres (2 to 4 hectares) of land. With small orchards and terraced gardening used to save the soil from erosion, farmers make as much as they can out of very little. In the country, men and women ride tractors or mules to the fields. Families share modern farm machinery, and many farmers still do much of the work by hand. They seed by hand, cultivate with a hoe, and harvest with a sickle or scythe. For larger fields, they use a plow, drawn by an ox or a mule, a method that has changed little since ancient times.

Most families tend flocks of goats and sheep. Both animals are used for their meat and milk. Their milk is used for cream, yogurt, and cheeses, which are usually made by hand. The sheep are also raised for their wool. As their ancestors did for centuries, some shepherds in the mountain regions live seminomadically. Bringing their flocks to higher pastures for the summer, the shepherds sleep in caves, huts, or under the stars.

During the growing season and the harvest, farmers bring their produce to the Saturday market. In the

This lab technician performs daily tests on grapes at the Boutari Winery. Greek wine experts use modern technology to ensure that the highest quality of wine will be produced. Wine is one of the country's most important agricultural exports and is integral to supporting local and national economies.

Shipping

Greece has a long maritime history. Ancient explorers and traders sailed as far west as Spain and into the Atlantic. Sailing along the French west coast, they reached as far north as England. Sailing east, they traded and settled along the Black Sea. During the Turkish domination, the Greeks were allowed to maintain their fleets as part of the Ottoman navy. When independence was declared, the Greek fleet was already assembled and ready to be used as a navy against the Turks.

The Greeks are still a powerful presence in shipping. There are many great Greek shipping families. Costas Lemos and his family control the largest merchant fleet in the world. Lemos spent seven years on ships, learning the business from the ground up. Savvy, shrewd, and decisive, Lemos has successfully weathered economic hard times. After World War II, shipping companies were waiting for new boats to be built. While others hesitated, Lemos ordered ships from the new Japanese builders. The Japanese built ships cheaper and faster. While the other shippers were waiting for boats, Lemos was back in business. He is the head of the Triton Shipping Company.

village square, they set up stalls to display their fruits and vegetables. In the fall, the farmers bring their grapes to the communal village winepress. In some villages, men still roll up their pants and women hold up their skirts to stomp the grapes with their bare feet.

In the winter, the women knit, weave, and embroider. They make pillowcases, rugs, and clothing. Bringing their products to the village square, they sell their goods to shops or tourists. The men spend the winter cleaning and repairing tools and equipment so that they will be ready for use in the spring.

Tourism

After the world wars and the civil wars, Greece was impoverished. Many Greeks could not make a living and felt forced to emigrate. The booming tourist industry has brought many of them home. Tourism needs many trades and workers to support it. The visitors need accommodations, guides, and equipment. On the islands, thousands of workers are needed for restaurants, hotels, suppliers, entertainment, tours, and transportation.

Since the 1990s, more than 10 million tourists visit Greece every year. The country draws visitors interested in history, archaeology, and art. With

The Hellenic Academy is located in Athens and provides educational programs for adult students. Specializing in modern Greek language courses, it makes available resources to those people wishing to learn Greek or improve their Greek language skills while acquiring a deeper acquaintance with Greece and its culture.

so many unspoiled mountains, forests, and bird sanctuaries, Greece attracts hunters, skiers, cyclists, and bird-watchers. On the islands, visitors can find everything from nature, sports, culture, history, and archaeology to pure leisure. The thousands of beaches vary from the white sands of Corfu to the black crushed-lava beaches on Santorini. The Greek people pride themselves on being gracious hosts. From the islands to the mainland, Greeks are proud of their country and eager to share it with the world.

GREECE
AT A GLANCE

HISTORY

The first great civilizations in Greece were the Bronze Age Cycladic, Minoan, and Mycenaean cultures. Cycladic culture flourished from around 2800 to 2300 BC until it was absorbed by the Minoan culture. The Minoan civilization reached its apex from 2200 to 1450 BC, until invaded by the Mycenaeans. The Minoan civilization was completely destroyed by 1400 BC. Invading mainland Greece between 2100 and 1900 BC, the Mycenaeans dominated much of the mainland and the Aegean Islands. Around 1200 BC, the Dorians invaded Greece and destroyed Mycenaean cities. This was the start of the Dark Ages, which spanned from 1200 to 800 BC, a bleak time of great upheaval. By 800 BC, Greece had emerged from the Dark Ages. As villages and cities organized into city-states, monarchies were replaced by aristocratic oligarchies. The Greek city-states worked to colonize the Mediterranean area. Between 593 and 510 BC, Solon and Cleisthenes introduced radical democratic reforms in Athens.

In 492 BC and 481 BC, the Persians invaded Greece and were decisively defeated both times. Athens founded the Delian League, a confederacy of Greek islands and city-states. The classical period, which lasted from 492 to 330 BC, was marked in the early years by astounding creativity in the arts and culture. Increasingly imperialistic, Athens fought Sparta and its allies in the Peloponnesian War (431–402 BC). Sparta won, but all of Greece was weakened by the long war. In 338 BC, Philip II of Macedonia defeated a coalition of Greek states, ending Greek freedom. After Philip's death six years later, his son Alexander the Great created an empire stretching from Europe and northern Africa, through the Middle East, and into Asia. After his death in 323 BC, Alexander's generals fought over the remains of his empire. In the first century BC, Greece became a province of the Roman Empire, and by the sixth century AD, it was a part of the Byzantine Empire. Over the next eleven centuries, Greece was repeatedly invaded and occupied. In 1453, the Turkish Ottoman Empire overthrew the Byzantine Empire. Though Greece attempted several revolts over the centuries, it remained under Turkish domination until the War of Independence, beginning in 1821.

After winning freedom from the Turks, Greece's political fate was decided by the European powers. Over the next 100 years, European nobles ruled Greece. Between 1913 and 1935, the brilliant Cretan statesman Eleuthérios Venizélos managed through treaties and alliances to reclaim regions of Greece. During World War II, Greece was invaded by Italians, Germans, and Bulgarians. Between 1944 and 1949, Greece experienced the agony of civil war in two Communist rebellions. Finally, between 1949 and 1964, there was a period of stability under Alexandros Papagos. This was followed by a series of unstable governments and a seven-year military junta. In 1974, a parliamentary republic was established and democracy was returned after more than 2,000 years. In 1981, the Panhellenic Socialist Movement claimed victory. Since 1995, Konstantinos Stephanopoulos has been head of state, and since 1996, Konstantinos Simitis has been prime minister.

ECONOMY

Greece has a mixed capitalistic economy. The public sector accounts for about one-half of the gross domestic product (GDP). Tourism is the key industry and accounts for a large part of the economy and foreign exchange earnings. Greece has the third largest shipping industry in the world. Other revenues are from industrial export and the trade and finance sectors. Greece joined the European Union (EU) in 1981. The major beneficiary of the EU, Greece receives funds from the EU equal to 4 percent of its GDP.

In recent years, the Greek government has been making concentrated and effective efforts to improve the economy. It successfully tightened economic policy to qualify for the January 1, 2001, deadline for entry into the European Economic and Monetary Union's (EMU) single currency program. The government cut the budget deficit to less than 2 percent of the GDP. Tightened monetary policy resulted in inflation falling from 20 percent in 1990 to 3.1 percent in 2000, which is the lowest rate in twenty-five years. In 2000, industrial production grew at 7 percent. Exports totaled $15.8 billion, and total imports were $33.9 billion. In 1998, the national budget had revenues of $45 billion and expenditures of $47.6 billion.

The Greek government has successfully transformed a depressed and wartorn country into an increasingly prosperous modern nation. Challenges for the future are reducing unemployment, continued restructuring of the economy, and privatizing leading state enterprises. Greece needs better public education, transport, and housing. Greece is also behind the rest of Europe in computerized record keeping, and its communication services need to be expanded. The government is searching for solutions to industrial and agricultural pollution, waste disposal, desertification, and dwindling water supplies. The government is making a concentrated effort to reduce smoking in its population. The government has helped to fund and build an oil pipeline to the Balkans. With aid to the new Balkan nations, Greece continues to support peace and stability in the area. Athens will host the 2004 Summer Olympic Games.

GOVERNMENT AND POLITICS

Greece is a presidential parliamentary republic. The present constitution was approved on June 11, 1975, and amended in March 1986. The parliament is a single-chamber legislative branch. The 300 members of the parliament are elected by popular vote and serve for four years. All Greek citizens over eighteen years old are required to vote. The government is led by the president, who is elected by the parliament for a five-year term. The present president, Konstantinos Stephanopoulos, was elected on February 2, 2000. The president chooses the prime minister from the political party receiving the most seats in the parliamentary election. The prime minister must then be approved by the parliament. The present prime minister, Konstantinos Simitis, was elected by a 90 percent vote.

The present political parties and their leaders are the Panhellenic Socialist Movement, led by Konstantinos Simitis; the Coalition of the Left and Progress, led by Nikolaos Konstandopoulos; the Communist Party, led by Aleka Papariga; the Democratic Social Movement, led by Dhimitrios Tsovolas; the New Democracy Conservatives, led by Konstandinos Karamanlis; the Political Spring, led by Antonis Samaras; and the Rainbow Coalition, led by Pavlos Voskopoulos.

The cabinet ministers are appointed by the president on the recommendation of the prime minister. There are eighteen cabinets or ministries, which include the Ministry of Economy and Finance, the Ministry of Foreign Affairs, the Ministry of National Defense, the Ministry of the Interior, the Ministry of Public Administration and Decentralization, the Ministry of Development, the Ministry of Environment, the Ministry of Physical Planning and Public Works, the Ministry of Education and Religious Affairs, the Ministry of Agriculture, the Ministry of Justice, the Ministry of Culture, the Ministry of Transport and Communication, the Ministry of Public Order, the Ministry of the Mercantile Marine, the Ministry of Press and Mass Media, the Ministry of Macedonia-Thrace, and the Ministry of the Aegean.

The Greek legal system is based on codified Roman law. The judiciary is divided into civil, criminal, and administrative courts. Judges for the Supreme Judicial Court and the Special Supreme Tribunal are appointed for life by the president after consultation with a judicial consul branch.

Greece is a charter member of the United Nations. It joined NATO (North Atlantic Treaty Organization) in 1952 and also belongs to many other European and world organizations. Greece has ongoing territorial disputes with Turkey over Cyprus and over maritime and air space. Greece dissented from supporting the NATO Alliance regarding troops in Kosovo. In the summer of 2002, the government finally had some success in arresting some of the 17 November (17N) terrorists. A radical leftist group, 17N is thought to be responsible for more than twenty assassinations of American, British, and Greek diplomats, military personnel, and businesspeople. The group's hatred of the United States can be traced back to the United States's backing of the oppressive military junta. Prior to the arrests, the United States had accused Greece of being soft on terrorism and threatened Greece with the loss of the 2004 Olympics.

TIMELINE

4000–3500 BC

Neolithic settlements in Greece.

1450 BC

Destruction of Minoan civilization.

1200–800 BC

Dorian invasion; Mycenaean cities destroyed; onset of Dark Ages.

900–725 BC

Geometric period; cultural reawakening; writing rediscovered; Greek trading posts throughout Mediterranean.

3500–1200 BC

Bronze Age civilizations: Mycenaean, Cycladic, and Minoan.

1460

Greece under Turkish rule; Venetians keep Ionian Islands.

1821

March 25, Greek independence declared; the War of Independence begins in 1821 and concludes in 1829.

1832

Greece is free; Prince Otho of Bavaria elected king.

1909–1936

Formation of Balkan League against Turkey; George I murdered; Eleuthérios Venizélos dominates Greek political life for three decades, steers Greece through Balkans Wars and first World War.

1914–1924

Greece enters war on Allied side; King Constantine elected; exchange of almost two million Greeks for 400,000 Turks.

1924–1935

King George II leaves; armed forces declare republic; military dictatorship followed by parliamentary rule under Venizélos.

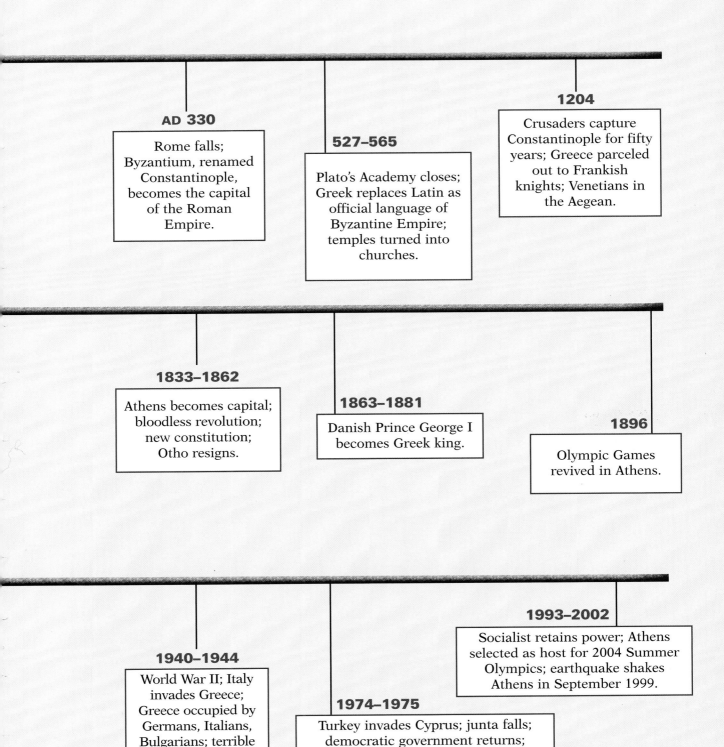

AD 330

Rome falls; Byzantium, renamed Constantinople, becomes the capital of the Roman Empire.

527–565

Plato's Academy closes; Greek replaces Latin as official language of Byzantine Empire; temples turned into churches.

1204

Crusaders capture Constantinople for fifty years; Greece parceled out to Frankish knights; Venetians in the Aegean.

1833–1862

Athens becomes capital; bloodless revolution; new constitution; Otho resigns.

1863–1881

Danish Prince George I becomes Greek king.

1896

Olympic Games revived in Athens.

1940–1944

World War II; Italy invades Greece; Greece occupied by Germans, Italians, Bulgarians; terrible famine.

1974–1975

Turkey invades Cyprus; junta falls; democratic government returns; republic proclaimed; new constitution.

1993–2002

Socialist retains power; Athens selected as host for 2004 Summer Olympics; earthquake shakes Athens in September 1999.

GREECE

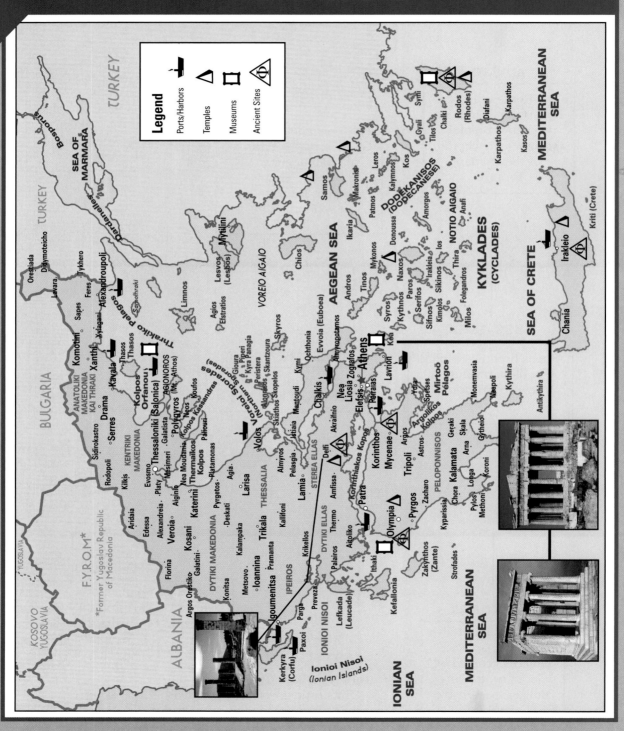

Legend

Ports/Harbors

Temples

Museums

Ancient Sites

TURKEY

Bosporus

SEA OF MARMARA

TURKEY

Dardanelles

Orestiada

Didymoteicho

Lavara

Tykhero

Sapes

Feres

Xylagani

Alexandroupoli

Samothraki

THRAKI

SEA OF MARMARA

ANATOLIKI MAKEDONIA KAI THRAKI

Komotini

Xanthi

Thasos

Thasos

Thraiko Pelagos

Limnos

Lesvos (Lesbos)

VOREIO AIGAIO

AEGEAN SEA

Agios Efstratios

Chios

Ikaria

Samos

Makronisi

Patmos

Leros

Kalymnos

Kos

DODEKANISOS (DODECANESE)

Tilos

Chalki

Symi

Rodos (Rhodes)

Gyali

Nisyros

Karpathos

Diafani

Kasos

MEDITERRANEAN SEA

NOTIO AIGAIO

Amorgos

Anafi

KYKLADES (CYCLADES)

Mykonos

Tinos

Andros

Syros

Kythnos

Serifos

Sifnos

Kimolos

Milos

Paros

Naxos

Donoussa

Iraklia

Irakleio

Ios

Sikinos

Thira

Folegandros

SEA OF CRETE

Chania

Kriti (Crete)

Irakleio

BULGARIA

Sidirokastro

Rodopoli

Serres

Drama

Kavala

Kolpos Orfanou

Kilkis

KENTRIKI MAKEDONIA

Thessaloniki (Salonica)

Galatista

AGIONOROS AGION OROS (Mt. Athos)

Poligyros

Kolpos Kassandras

Paliouri

Neos Marmaras

Kolpos Toronaios

Skiathos

Skopelos

Alonnisos

Skantzoura

Voreioi Sporades (Northern Sporades)

Gioura

Piperi

Kyra Panagia

Peristera

Pelagonisi

Skyros

Achthonia

Evvoia (Euboea)

Mantoudi

Kymi

Istiaia

Kyllini

FYROM*

*Former Yugoslav Republic of Macedonia

YUGOSLAVIA

KOSOVO YUGOSLAVIA

Argos Orestiko

Kastoria

Galatini

Florina

Edessa

Aridaia

Alexandreia

Veroia

Aiginio

Platy

Nea Moudania

Msimeri

Thermaikos Kolpos

Platamonas

Katerini

Pyrgetos

Deskati

Agia

DYTIKI MAKEDONIA

Kosani

Kalampaka

Trikala

Larisa

THESSALIA

Kallifoni

Lamia

Almyros

Pelasgia

Volos

Pagasitikos Kolpos

Evosmo

Konitsa

Metsovo

Ioannina

Igoumenitsa

Paxoi

Parga

Preveza

IPEIROS

Iramanta

Kifellos

Krikellos

DYTIKI ELLAS

Palairos

Thermo

Aitoliko

Patra

Pyrgos

Olympia

Zacharo

Kyparissia

Pylos

Methoni

Koroni

Chora

Kalamata

Longa

Arna

Skala

Gytheio

Monemvasia

Neapoli

Kythira

Antikythira

PELOPONNISOS

Tripoli

Astros

Geraki

Argos

Mycenae

Argolikos Kolpos

Korinthos

STEREA ELLAS

Delfi

Amfissa

Korinthiakos Kopos

Akraifnio

Nea Liosia

Zoglafos

Elefsis

Athens

Peiraias

Lavrion

Kea

Spetses

Ydra

Mirtoö Pélagos

ALBANIA

Kerkyra (Corfu)

IONIOI NISOI

Lefkada (Leucade)

Ithaki

Kefallonia

Zakynthos (Zante)

Strofades

Ionioi Nisoi (Ionian Islands)

IONIAN SEA

MEDITERRANEAN SEA

MEDITERRANEAN SEA

ECONOMIC FACT SHEET

GDP in U.S. dollars: $201.1 billion

GDP Sectors: Agriculture 7.6%, industry 21.2%, services 71.2%

Land Use: Arable land 19%, permanent crops 8%, irrigated land 10%, forests 20%, pastures 41%, national parks 3.6%, other 12%

Currency: Euros per US dollar: 1.13 (January 2002)

Workforce: 4.32 million; trade and services 59%; industry 21%; agriculture, forestry, and fishing 20%

Major Agricultural Products: Wheat, corn, barley, sugar beets, olives, tomatoes, wine, tobacco, potatoes, dairy products

Major Exports: $12.6 billion; manufactured goods, food, beverages, petroleum products

Major Imports: $31.4 billion; manufactured goods, foodstuffs, fuels, chemicals

Significant Trading Partners:

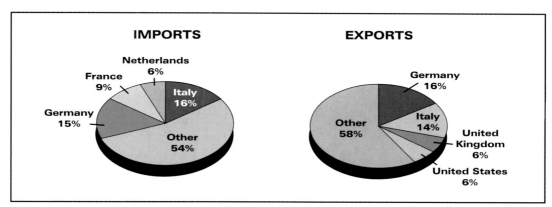

IMPORTS
Netherlands 6%
France 9%
Germany 15%
Italy 16%
Other 54%

EXPORTS
Germany 16%
Italy 14%
United Kingdom 6%
United States 6%
Other 58%

Rate of Unemployment: 11.3%

Highways: 72,703 miles (117,000 km)

Railroads: 1,537 miles (2,571 km)

Waterways: 50 miles (80 km)

Airports: 79; New Athens airport at Spata opened in 2001

POLITICAL FACT SHEET

Official Country Name:
Hellenic Republic

System of Government:
Presidential parliamentary
republic

Federal Structure: One-
chamber parliament; executive
branch of president, prime
minister, and eighteen cabi-
nets; and judiciary branch of civil, administrative, and criminal courts

Official Flag: Nine equal horizontal stripes of blue alternating with white; a
blue square in the upper-left corner bearing a white cross; the cross symbolizes
Greek Orthodoxy, the established religion of the country. Flag adopted
December 22, 1978.

National Anthem: "Hymn to Freedom," words by Dionysius Solomós (1798–
1857), music by Nikolaos Mantzaros (1795–1873). Adopted 1864.

I recognize thee by the edge
Of thy terrible sword,
I recognize thee by the countenance
That with violence measures the earth.

Spring from the sacred
Bones of the Greeks,
Valorous, as at first
Hail, Hail, O Freedom!

Percentage of Voters: 100%. Voting in Greece is mandatory by every citizen
age eighteen years or older.

CULTURAL FACT SHEET

Official Languages: Greek, English

Major Religions: Greek Orthodox 98%, Islam 1.3%, other 0.7%

Capital: Athens

Population: 10,645,343

Ethnic Groups: Greek 98%, other 2%

Life Expectancy: 76.03 male, 81.32 female

Time: GMT+0200

Literacy Rate: 98%

National Flower: Violet

Cultural Leaders:
>**Visual Arts:** Foots Kondoglou, Jiannis Spyropoulos, Christos Caras
>**Literature:** Costas Montis, Aristotelis P. Tsakonas, Alexis Stamatis, Rhea Galanaki
>**Music:** Mikis Theodorakis, Dino Mastroyiannis
>**Entertainment:** Michael Cacoyannis, Irene Pappas, Vangelis Theodoropoulos
>**Sports:** Heidi Antkatzides, Takis Lemonis, Nikos Kaklamanakis

National Holidays and Festivals

The majority of these holidays fall on a different day each year. These dates reflect the 2003 calendar year.

January 1: **New Year's Day**	May 1: **Labor Day**
January 6: **Epiphany**	June 4: **White Monday**
March 25: **Independence Day**	August 15: **Feast of the Assumption**
March 26: **Ash Monday**	
April 13: **Good Friday**	October 28: **National Holiday**
April 15: **Easter**	December 25: **Christmas**
April 16: **Easter Monday**	December 26: **Boxing Day**

Working Life: Typical workweek: Monday to Friday, 7:30 AM–3 PM (May to September), 8 AM–3:30 PM (October to May). Average hours worked per week: 40.

Annual time off per year: 32 to 34 days

GLOSSARY

Acropolis (uh-KROP-uh-lis) Literally means "high point." A high rocky outcropping used as a center for defense. Originally the site of fortresses and the residences of kings, the Athenian Acropolis was the ceremonial and religious center of the city.

axiom (AK-see-um) A statement universally accepted as true, or an established principle.

bouzouki (boo-ZOO-kee) A mandolin-like stringed instrument used to accompany folk songs and dancers.

desertification (deh-zert-uh-fuh-KAY-shun) Change of arable land into desert.

harem (HAR-em) The part of a Muslim household where all the women, wives, concubines, and female servants lived.

hierarchical (hi-er-AR-kih-kul) Referring to a hierarchy, groups of people arranged in order of rank, as in church government.

imperialistic (im-peer-ee-uh-LIS-tik) Referring to imperialism, seeking to dominate the economic or political affairs of weaker countries.

impiety (im-PIE-uh-tee) Lack of reverence for God.

Indo-European (IN-doh-yoor-uh-PEE-an) A people thought to have come from Eurasia, and the language of these people. Decendants of the Indo-European family of languages are spoken throughout the world, extending from Iceland to Bangladesh. Traces of it appear in Persian, Hindi, Sanskrit, and all European languages.

junta (HUN-tuh) A group of military men in power often after a government overthrow.

maritime (MAR-ih-tym) Relating to sea navigation or shipping.

martyr (MART-er) A person who chooses suffering or death rather than give up his or her faith or principles; to be tortured or killed for one's beliefs.

Panaceia (pan-uh-SAY-uh) Goddess of remedies and herbal preparations, daughter of Asclepius, god of health; "panacea" means "cure-all."

scribe (SKRYB) Someone who made copies of ancient manuscripts.

seismic (SYZ-mik) Having to do with earthquakes.

Titans (TY-tenz) Early race of giant Greek deities overthrown by Olympic gods.

trident (TRY-dent) A three-pronged spear.

FOR MORE INFORMATION

Canadian Embassy in Greece
41 Gennadiou Street
Athens, Greece 115 21
e-mail: athns@dfait-maeci.gc.ca

Consulate General
1170 Place du Frere Andre
Montreal, PQ H3B 3C6
Canada
(514) 875-8781

Greek Embassy
80 Maclaren Street
Ottawa, ON K2P OK6
(613) 238-6271

Hellenic Folklore Society
606 Greendale Road
Glenview, IL 60025
(847) 657-0958
e-mail: orpheus@ohfs.org

Hellenic Society "Paideia," Inc.
P.O. Box 818
20 Dog Lane
Storrs, CT 06268
(860) 429-8518

Metropolitan Museum of Art
1000 Fifth Avenue
New York, NY 10028-0198
(212) 535-7710
Web site: http://www.metmuseum.org

Pancretan Association of America
3843 Wallings Road
North Royalton, OH 44133
(216) 237-0257

United States Embassy in Greece
Ambassador Thomas J. Miller
91 Vassilisis Sophias Avenue
10160 Athens, Greece
+ 30 10 210-721-2951
e-mail: usembasssy@usembassy.gr
Web site:
http://www.usembassy.gr/sitemap.htm

Web Sites

Due to the changing nature of Internet
links, the Rosen Publishing Group, Inc., has
developed an online list of Web sites related
to the subject of this book. This site is
updated regularly. Please use this link to
access the list:

http://www.rosenlinks.com/pswc/gree

FOR FURTHER READING

Gianakoulis, Theodore. *The Land and People of Greece*. Philadelphia: J. B. Lippincott Company, 1972.

Hull, Robert E. *Everyday Life: World of Ancient Greece*. Danbury, CT: Grolier Publishing, 1999.

Pearson, Anne. *Ancient Greece*. New York: Alfred A. Knopf, 1992.

Powell, Anton. *Ancient Greece*. New York: Facts on File, 1989.

Renault, Mary. *The Lion in the Gateway*. New York: Harper & Row, 1964.

Sutcliff, Rosemary. *The Wanderings of Odysseus*. New York: Delacorte Press, 1995.

Tavlarios, Irene. *Greek Food and Drink*. New York: The Bookwright Press, 1988.

Williams, Susan. *The Greeks*. New York: Thomson Learning, 1993.

BIBLIOGRAPHY

Andrews, Kevin. *The Flight of Ikaros: A Journey into Greece*. Cambridge, England: The Riverside Press, 1959.

Constantelos, Demetrios J. *The Greek Orthodox Church: Faith, History, and Practice*. New York: The Seabury Press, 1967.

Eliot, Alexander. *The Horizon Concise History of Greece*. New York: American Heritage Publishing Co., Inc., 1972.

Elytis, Odysseus. *The Collected Poems of Odysseus Elytis*. Jeffrey Carson and Likos Sarris, trans. Baltimore: The Johns Hopkins University Press, 1997.

Gage, Nicholas. *Hellas: A Portrait of Greece*. New York: Villard Books, l986.

Gidal, Sonia, and Tim Gidal. *My Village in Greece*. New York: Random House, 1960.

Graves, Robert. *The Greek Myths: Volume 1*. Middlesex, England: Penguin Books, 1984.

Graves, Robert. *The Greek Myths: Volume 2*. Middlesex, England: Penguin, 1984.

Hamilton, Edith. *The Echo of Greece*. New York: W. W. Norton & Company, 1957.

Hamilton, Edith. *The Greek Way*. New York: W. W. Norton & Company, 1964.

Humez, Alexander, and Nicholas Humez. *Alpha to Omega: The Life & Times of the Greek Alphabet*. Boston: David R. Godine, Publisher, Inc., 1986.

Hyde, Walter W. *Greek Religion and Its Survivals*. New York: Cooper Square Publishers, Inc., 1963.

Keeley, Edmund, and Peter Bien, ed. *Modern Greek Writers*. Princeton, NJ: Princeton University Press, 1972.

Leacroft, Helen, and Richard Leacroft. *The Buildings of Ancient Greece*. Reading, MA: Addison-Wesley, 1976.

Sheldon, Peter. *The American Express Pocket Guide to Greece*. New York: Simon and Schuster, 1983.

Thucydides. *The Peloponnesian War*. Rex Warner, trans. Middlesex, England: Penguin Books, 1970.

Yianilos, Theresa Karas. *The Complete Greek Cookbook*. New York: Avenel Books, 1970.

Zane, Eva. *Greek Cooking for the Gods*. San Francisco: 101 Productions, 1970.

WEB SITES

Ball, Philip. Nature. "Oracle's Secret Fault Found." July 17, 2001. Retrieved June 13, 2002 (http://www.nature.com).

CreteTravel.com. "Currency Converter for Euro Guide." Retrieved August 12, 2002 (http://www.cretetravel.com).

Edelstein, Ludwig. "Nova Online." 2001. Retrieved August 14, 2002 (http://www.pbs.org).

EIROnline. September 3, 2002. Retrieved September 15, 2002 (http://www.eiro.eurofound.ie).

Embassy of Greece. "Geography." Retrieved September 10, 2002 (http://www.greekembassy.org).

Embassy of Greece. "Greek Foreign Policy." Retrieved September 10, 2002 (http://www.greekembassy.org).

Global Sources. "Travel Center." Retrieved September 13, 2002 (http://www.globalsources.com).

Greece for Visitors. "Greek Political Parties and Politicians." Retrieved September 12, 2002 (http://gogreece.about.com).

Greece Now. "Culture." Retrieved September 15, 2002 (http://www.greece.gr).

Greece Now. "Generation of Optimists." Retrieved June 27, 2002 (http://www.greece.gr).

Greece Now. "Olympics Go to School." Retrieved June 24, 2002 (http://www.greece.gr).

Hellenic Ministry of Culture. "The Cultural Olympiad." 2001. Retrieved August 16, 2002 (http://www.culture.gr).

International Idea Institute for Democracy and Electoral Assistance. "Greece." Retrieved September 13, 2002 (http://idea.int).

Nobel E-Museum. "George Seferis-Nobel Lecture." October 19, 2001. Retrieved June 22, 2002 (http://www.nobel.se).

Olympic Creed. Retrieved August 13, 2002 (http://www.personal.psu.ed).

Plagiarist.com. "C. P. Cavafy."
Retrieved August 22, 2002
(http://www.plagiarist.com).

Roach, John. "Delphic Oracle's Lips May
Have Been Loosened by Gas Vapors."
National Geographic News, August
14, 2001. Retrieved June 13, 2002
(http://news.nationalgeographic.com).

TUC Online. "Employment Research."
Retrieved September 13, 2002
(http://www.tuc.org.uk).

World Fact Book. "Greece." January 1,
2002. Retrieved September 13, 2002
(http://www.cia.gov).

PRIMARY SOURCE IMAGE LIST

Page 7: Now located at the British Museum in London, England, this sculpture of the head of the horse of Selene's chariot dates from 438 to 432 BC.

Page 9: The coin seen on this page, a silver drachma of Philip II, king of Macedon, was minted at Pella in 354 BC.

Page 17: This detail of the Dolphin Fresco, dating between 1600 and 1400 BC, is located at the Palace of Knossos in Crete, Greece.

Page 18: The Treaty of Alliance between Crete, Lycos, and Rhodes dates from the second century BC. It is housed at the Archaeological Museum of Venice in Venice, Italy.

Page 19 (top): This artifact, a gold death mask of Agamemnon, dates from between 1580 and 1500 BC. It is located at the National Archaeological Museum in Athens, Greece.

Page 19 (bottom): This fifth-century BC Greek vase is now located at the Louvre Museum in Paris, France.

Page 20: This bronze statue of the charioteer of Delphi dates from 474 BC. It is now located at the Archaeological Museum in Delphi, Greece.

Page 21: These ceramic tablets date from the fifth century BC. They are housed at the Museum of Ancient Agora in Athens, Greece.

Page 22: This marble fragment of a kleroterion dates from the third century BC. It is now located at the Museum of Ancient Agora in Athens, Greece.

Page 23: The statue of Demeter seen on this page dates from between the sixth and fifth centuries BC. It is now located in the Archaeological Museum of Syracuse in Syracuse, Sicily.

Page 24: The illustration pictured here was taken from a thirteenth-century Seljuk manuscript *The Best Maxims and Most Precious Dictums of Al-Mubashir*. The original is housed at the Topkapi Museum in Istanbul, Turkey.

Page 25: The Tumulus of Marathon in Attica, Greece, was erected in 490 BC.

Page 26: This original oil flask dates from 475 to 420 BC. It is now housed at the Museum of Mediterranean Archeology in Marseilles, France.

Page 27: The mosaic seen in this photograph, a work titled *Battle of Issus*, dates from the late second century BC. It is housed at the National Archaeological Museum in Naples, Italy.

Page 28: This engraving of a Greek revolutionary raising the flag of rebellion is housed at the Musée des Arts Décoratifs in Paris, France.

Page 29: This painting of the Battle of Navarino is located at the Museen der Stadt Wien in Karlsplatz, Vienna, Austria.

Page 30: This photograph was taken in Kyrenia, Cyprus, on July 20, 1974.

Page 32: This undated photograph was taken in Rome, Italy.

Page 36 (top): This artifact, known as the Phaistos Disc, dates from 1650 BC and was created by the Minoans. It is now housed at the Archaeological Museum of Herakleion in Crete, Greece.

Page 36 (bottom): The second-century BC stone tablet seen in this photograph was created by the Mycenaeans. It is now housed at the National Archaeological Museum in Athens, Greece.

Page 39: This photograph of Giorgos Seferis was taken in 1965.

Page 41: This bronze Etruscan sculpture titled *The Wounded Chimera of Arezzo* dates from the fourth century BC. It is now housed at the National Archaeological Museum in Florence, Italy.

Page 42: The relief sculpture of Apollo and Poseidon from the Parthenon dates from 440 to 432 BC. It is now housed at the Acropolis Museum in Athens, Greece.

Page 43: This terra-cotta Lefkandi Centaur dates from 900 BC. It is located at the Archaeology Museum of Eretria in Eretria, Greece.

Page 44: This red-figure vase by Master of Niobids dates from 460 BC. It is now housed at the National Archaeological Museum of Spina in Ferrara, Italy.

Page 45: The Temple of Apollo at Delphi in Delphi, Greece, dates from the fourth century BC.

Page 46: This cup with an illustration of Amphytrite, Athena, and Theseus was made by Euphronius and attributed to Panaitios. It dates from the sixth century BC and is housed at the Louvre Museum in Paris, France.

Page 47: This illustration from the Greek manuscript *De animalium propietate libellus* dates from the sixteenth century. It is now housed at the Biblioteca Nazionale Marciana in Venice, Italy.

Page 48: This statue of Zeus is located at the Museo Pio Clementino in Vatican City, Italy.

Page 55: This black-figure vase dates from the sixth century BC.

Page 56: This seventh-century painting titled *Virgin and Child* was created by Emmanuel Zane. The original can be found in the collections of the Byzantine Museum in Athens, Greece.

Page 58 (top): The Byzantine fresco of Christ Pantocrator seen here was completed between 1072 and 1078. It is located at the Basilica San Angelo in Formis, Capua, Italy.

Page 58 (bottom): This Byzantine illustration of the Psalm of David dates from 1066 and was written and illustrated by Theodoros of Caesarea. The original is now housed at the British Library in London, England.

Page 61: This Byzantine fresco of the miracle of Jesus Christ curing a man born blind dates from 1072. It is located at the Basilica of San Angelo in Formis, Capua, Italy.

Page 64: The marble bust of Socrates seen on this page is located at the Archaeological Museum in Naples, Italy.

Page 65: The marble relief seen on this page dates from the second century BC and is located at the Archaeological Museum in Piraeus, Greece.

Page 66: This is an illustration from a medieval Greek manuscript.

Page 68: The Minoan fresco in this photograph dates from 1500 BC. It is located in Santorini, Greece.

Page 69: This red-figure vase is dated 750 BC and is located at the Archaeological Museum in Argos, Greece.

Page 71 (top): This marble sculpture, *Sulking Kore*, dates from 480 BC. It is located at the Acropolis Museum in Athens, Greece.

Page 72: The Parthenon in Athens, Greece, was constructed between 477 and 438 BC.

Page 73: The theater at Epidauros, Greece, was built during the fourth century BC by Polykleitos.

Page 74: This Byzantine mosaic of Pentecost dates from the early eleventh century. It is located at the Hosios Loukas Monastery in Boeotia, Greece.

Page 75: El Greco painted this oil painting, entitled *Coronation of the Virgin*, in 1591. It is housed at the Santa Cruz Museum in Toledo, Spain.

Page 77: This engraved floor plan of the House of the Faun by Fausto and Felice Niccolini is part of a manuscript titled *Le case i monumenti di Pompei* (Houses and Monuments of Pompeii) and dates from between 1854 and 1890. The original is housed at the Musée des Arts Décoratifs in Paris, France.

Page 79: This Pitsa Tablet, made of wood, dates from 470 BC. It is located at the National Archaeological Museum in Athens, Greece.

Page 80: Column IV of the only surviving manuscript of the Athenian Constitution, seen on this page, was written by Aristotle in 350 BC and found in an Egyptian papyrus. It is now located at the British Museum in London, England.

Page 81: This marble relief of a Roman sarcophagus dates from 150 BC. It is now located at the Louvre Museum in Paris, France.

Page 82 (top): This marble bust of Aeschylus is located at the Capitoline Museum in Rome, Italy.

Page 84 (bottom): This marble bust of Sophocles is located at the Römisch Germanisches Museum in Cologne, Germany.

Page 83 (top): This bust of Euripides dates from 1620. It is located at the Ny Carlsberg Glyptothek in Copenhagen, Denmark.

Page 83 (bottom): This eighth-century BC bronze tympanon is located at the Archaeological Museum in Heraikleion, Greece.

Page 86: This portrait of Odysseus Elytis was taken in 1979 in Athens, Greece.

Page 87: This photograph of Mikis Theodorakis was taken in 1977 in Athens, Greece.

INDEX

About the Author

Maura McGinnis is a singer, composer, lyricist, and teacher. She lives in the Hudson Valley with a cat, a dog, and a horse.

Designer: Geri Fletcher; **Cover Designer:** Tahara Hasan; **Editor:** Joann Jovinelly; **Photo Researcher:** Gillian Harper; **Photo Research Assistant:** Fernanda Rocha